DISCARD

BUT NOW I SEE

The
White
Southern
Racial
Conversion
Narrative

FRED HOBSON

Louisiana State University Press
Baton Rouge

Copyright © 1999 by Louisiana State University Press
All rights reserved
Manufactured in the United States of America
First printing
08 07 06 05 04 03 02 01 00 99   5 4 3 2 1

Designer: Michele Myatt Quinn
Typeface: Adobe Garamond
Typesetter: Coghill Composition
Printer and binder: Edwards Brothers, Inc.

Library of Congress Cataloging-in-Publication Data

Hobson, Fred C., 1943–
    But now I see : the white southern racial conversion narrative /
Fred Hobson.
        p.   cm. — (The Walter Lynwood Fleming lectures in southern
history)
    Includes bibliographical references (p.   ) and index.
    ISBN 0-8071-2384-6 (alk. paper). — ISBN 0-8071-2410-9 (pbk. :
alk. paper)
    1. Whites—Southern States—Biography.   2. Autobiography.
3. Whites—Southern States—Attitudes.   4. Racism—Southern States—
Psychological aspects.   5. Conversion.   6. Southern States—Race
relations.   I. Title.   II. Series.
    F220.A1H63   1999
    810.9'975—dc21   98-50180
                                                       CIP

Portions of this book appeared previously in different form as "The Sins of the Fathers: Lillian Smith and Katharine Du Pre Lumpkin" in *Southern Review,* Vol. 34, No. 4 (Autumn, 1998); and "The Southern Racial Conversion Narrative: Larry L. King and Pat Watters," in *Virginia Quarterly Review,* Vol. 75, No. 2 (Spring, 1999).

The paper in this book meets the guidelines for permanence and durability of the Committee on Production Guidelines for Book Longevity of the Council on Library Resources. ∞

For Jane and Alice

For Bob and Lillian Tuttle

I once was lost, but now am found
Was blind, but now I see.

—"Faith's Review and Expectation" ("Amazing Grace"),
    by John Newton, English minister, abolitionist,
    and former slave ship captain

Contents

PREFACE

THIS BOOK IS an outgrowth both of reading I have done in the Puritan conversion narrative of the seventeenth and early eighteenth centuries and of my own earlier work in southern literature and intellectual history. In *Tell About the South: The Southern Rage to Explain,* I treated at length two broad groups of white southern writers divided largely over the issue of race—groups I termed the southern party of remembrance and the party of shame and guilt. Over the course of my research for *Tell About the South,* I noticed that a number of white southerners in the 1940s, 1950s, 1960s, and 1970s had written books, either autobiographies or very personal social commentaries (or both), in which they attempted to come to terms with racial guilt—their own and their region's. In that study I was able to treat only two of those writers, Lillian Smith and James McBride Dabbs, and Smith and Dabbs more briefly than I would like liked. An invitation from the Department of History at Louisiana State University to deliver the Walter Lynwood Fleming Lectures in April 1998—as well as a leave of absence in the fall of 1997 from the University of North Carolina at Chapel Hill—gave me an opportunity to examine more fully Smith, Dabbs, and a number of other white southerners who wrote what I came to call racial conversion narratives.

My greatest debts, then, are to Louisiana State University and the University of North Carolina at Chapel Hill. I was honored by the invitation to deliver the Fleming Lectures, and I was gratified as well, since a trip to Baton Rouge meant a return to a place I had spent three of the most productive and enjoyable years of my professional life. I can hardly count my debts to Lewis P. Simpson, and I owe much also to other friends and scholars at LSU, particularly James Olney, John Lowe, Paul Paskoff, Peggy W. Prenshaw, Anne Loveland, William Cooper, Gaines Foster, and Michael Griffith. I am grateful as well to the Louisiana State University Press, particularly Les Phillabaum, John Easterly, Nicola Mason, and Barbara Outland. My debts to the University of North Carolina are equally great, to the University for the Kenan Leave which enabled me to write the lectures that resulted in this book, to the interlibrary loan staff of the Walter Royal Davis Library, and to the following individuals: William Andrews, Laurence Avery, Frances Coombs, Joseph Flora, Darryl Gless, Philip Gura, Jacquelyn Dowd Hall, Kimball King, George Lensing, Cindy Peterson, Jack Raper, Louis Rubin, and Nina Wallace.

I am especially grateful to Barbara Bennett, John Egerton, Elliott Gorn, and Sally Green for sharing their expertise, counsel, editorial skills, and time. I wish to thank the following persons as well for their assistance: Staige Blackford, William Boring, Bruce Clayton, Ambrose Dudley, Vince Fitzpatrick, Beth Furr, Judy Gehrig, Rose Gladney, Jane Hobson (I and II), Linda Whitney Hobson, Charles F. Irons, Wayne Pond, Scott Romine, John Rusher and Elizabeth Spencer, Graham Snyder, Jane and Fred White, and Lola Williams, and Sally Wolff.

Chapel Hill
August 1998

BUT NOW I SEE

INTRODUCTION

Of Guilt and Shame, Race and Repentance

THE TERM "CONVERSION NARRATIVE," at least in American letters, usually refers to a particular form of expression arising in New England in the seventeenth century—either such written works as Cotton Mather's lengthy *Paterna* and Jonathan Edwards' much briefer "Personal Narrative" or, more narrowly defined, that oral confession of sins by ordinary men and women, usually delivered before a church congregation, a confession heard and recorded by a minister and which, if the candidate were judged worthy, resulted in "conversion" and church membership.[1] In that sense, the purely religious, the confession narrative belongs to a rather remote history. In quite another sense, however—in the realm of the secular—the term might be used, particularly in the American South, to describe a much more recent phenomenon, indeed a form of southern self-expression not seen *until* the 1940s. I have in mind certain autobiographies or works of highly personal social commentary by Lillian Smith, Katharine Du Pre Lumpkin, James McBride Dabbs, Sarah Patton Boyle, Will Campbell, Willie Morris, Larry L. King, Pat Watters, and other white southerners, works written over the past half-century which qualify as *racial* conversion narratives—that is,

---

1. See, on Puritan conversion narrative, Patricia Caldwell, *The Puritan Conversion Narrative: The Beginnings of American Expression* (New York, 1983); Charles Lloyd Cohen, *God's Caress: The Psychology of Puritan Religious Experience* (New York, 1986); Peter A. Dorsey, *Sacred Estrangement: The Rhetoric of Conversion in Modern American Autobiography* (University Park, Pa., 1993); C. C. Goen, Introduction to *The Great Awakening*, by Jonathan Edwards (New Haven, 1972); and Philip F. Gura, *A Glimpse of Sion's Glory: Puritan Radicalism in New England, 1620–1660* (Middletown, Conn., 1984).

works in which the authors, all products of and willing participants in a harsh, segregated society, confess racial wrongdoings and are "converted," in varying degrees, from racism to something approaching racial enlightenment. Indeed the language of most of these white southerners is the language of religious conversion—"sin," "guilt," "blindness," "seeing the light," "repentance," "redemption," and so forth. Such an occurrence is hardly surprising when one considers that conversion, in a purely religious sense, has been so much a part of the life of the Calvinist South and that nearly all of the writers mentioned above came out of a strong religious tradition. Many of them, at the time they wrote, had left the church—at least the church of their fathers—but all seemed to have retained the habit of seeking redemption, even if of a secular variety. Departing from the old vertical southern religion—that salvation-centered faith with heaven as its goal[2]—they embraced a horizontal religion which held that getting right with man was at least as important as getting right with God.

Before turning to these particular southerners, and to the larger matter of southern racial repentance, I want to look briefly at the New England conversion narrative and consider its particular characteristics. Of course, the kind of autobiographical writing that could be labeled "conversion narrative" goes back far earlier than the Puritans, at least as far back as the *Confessions* of St. Augustine, and even further. Almost all conversion narratives, religious or secular, bear essentially the same form—the description of a journey from darkness (the "dark shadows," in Augustine's words) to light, from sinfulness to a recognition of sin and consequently a changed life. As concerns the Puritans in particular, the narratives of Mather and Edwards, as all such Calvinist narratives, begin with an acknowledgment of personal sin. Mather proclaims himself (with somewhat more creativity than most of the later southerners) "a Wretched, Filthy, Loathsome Creature," and Edwards refers to the "bottomless depths of secret corruption and deceit" in his heart, the "infinite depths of wickedness, pride [and] hypocrisy": he was "the very worst of all mankind; of all that have been, since the beginning of the world, to this time," and one deserving of "by far the lowest place in hell." (Another Puritan, Michael Wigglesworth, also proclaimed *himself*

---

2. See Samuel S. Hill, Jr., *Southern Churches in Crisis* (New York, 1966), 106.

"the chief of sinners," a "poor sinful worm.")[3] Of course, there existed among the Puritans a kind of hierarchy, an aristocracy of sinfulness, and each Puritan tried to surpass the other in a profession of wretchedness, the assumption seeming to be the greater the sinner the greater the potential saint—and the greater God's grace in transforming his life. Such pride in one's earlier transgressions was, after all, in the tradition of St. Paul, who had also proclaimed himself the greatest of sinners.

After the recognition of one's sinful nature—a feeling of extreme misery, unworthiness, and despair (being "laid low" as some Puritans termed it)— came a period, in Mather's words, of "unspeakable Horror and Anger" at one's "Spiritual Sins," and then, either abruptly or gradually, a vision of God's grace and the possibility of change in one's life. "In some," Edwards wrote in his "Faithful Narrative" of the Northampton revivals of 1734– 1735, "converting light is like a glorious brightness suddenly shining in upon a person," who is thus "brought out of darkness into marvellous light." After earlier having "their consciences . . . suddenly smitten as if their hearts were pierced through with a dart," sinners were prepared to move from "conviction" (or a full awareness of sin) to conversion. Parts of the process were often accompanied, as Mather wrote of himself, by a "Flood of Tears." One became, finally, a changed being, "renouncing the old self and reconstructing a new one"—but a new one, being human, given to backsliding.[4]

The Puritan's experience of his or her conversion—or "turning" as it was called—and the desire to convey to a reader as much of that experience as possible was, Ronald A. Bosco has written, "the central impulse in all Puritan autobiographical endeavors." As Jonathan Edwards maintained, conversion "change[s] the heart, and infuse[s] life into the dead soul," and the result is "spiritual delight" and "unparalleled joy." With conversion, C. C. Goen has written, "love displaced fear and furnished a new ground of con-

---

3. Cotton Mather, *Paterna: The Autobiography of Cotton Mather,* ed. Ronald A. Bosco (Delmar, N.Y., 1976), 119; Jonathan Edwards, "Personal Narrative," in *Jonathan Edwards: Basic Writings,* ed. Ola Elizabeth Winslow (New York, 1966), 86, 95, 94; and the Introduction to *The Diary of Michael Wigglesworth 1653–1657,* ed. Edmund S. Morgan (Gloucester, Mass., 1965), vi.

4. Mather, *Paterna,* 13–14; Edwards, "A Faithful Narrative," in *The Great Awakening,* 177–78, 122; Mather, *Paterna,* 119; and Cohen, *God's Caress,* 15.

fidence"; sinners acquired new identities, and as a consequence "social conflicts were healed and people were united," in Edwards' words, in "affection one to another."[5]

This, in brief, was the Puritan conversion narrative of the seventeenth and early eighteenth centuries, and it is obvious, as I suggested earlier, that the kind of conversion I wish to investigate is different from that experience in many respects. Not only am I dealing principally with salvation of a secular sort—the end of which is human brotherhood, rather than getting to heaven—but one finds in these secular converts little fear (at least consciously expressed) of Satan and hell. One finds, in most cases, no minister as mentor, shepherding the convert on his or her way; rather the potential convert observes the world around him, heeds an inner voice, and crosses the line on his own, in the process (quite contrary to the Puritan result of membership in the church/state) leaving behind the established southern order, religious and otherwise, as well as the southern white community in a more inclusive sense. Finally, of course, the sins repented of are more "social" than "personal" (although, of course, at base all sins are personal), and sins, as well, acknowledged and confessed not only for oneself but for one's family, one's community, and one's homeland.

What these southern "conversion narratives" have in common with the Puritan narratives, however, is a recognition and confession of the writer's own sins and the announced need for redemption, as well as a description of the writer's radical transformation—a sort of secular salvation. But the guilt that motivates the confession—the "conviction" of sin, as the Puritans termed it—is no less real, nor is the deep need to tell one's story, nor the changed lives that these narratives relate. The impulse is the same—to witness, to testify. Indeed, the writing of a conversion narrative is, to a great extent, the final proof of that conversion—the equivalent of testifying. Confession, of course, is not synonymous with conversion, but confession is a major step in that direction—and, to view the matter in general or nonliterary terms, one is struck by the extent of white racial confession in the public life of the South over the past few decades: George Wallace confess-

5. Bosco, Introduction to Mather's *Paterna*, xxxv; Edwards, "A Narrative of Surprising Conversions," in *Jonathan Edwards on Revival* (1984), 40; and Goen (also Goen quoting Edwards), Introduction to Edwards' *The Great Awakening*, 32.

ing his racism, apologizing and asking forgiveness of John Lewis, Jesse Jackson, the members of the Dexter Avenue Baptist Church, and nearly anyone else who will listen; former Arkansas schoolgirl Hazel Bryan publicly apologizing for her verbal abuse of Elizabeth Eckford and the other black students who enrolled at Little Rock's Central High School in 1957; even the Southern Baptist Convention apologizing for its institutional racism. Most southern racial conversions have come not in a single impulse, as religious conversions, often induced by religious revivals, tend to. And the racial conversion narrative, in written form, seems to lack the *ritual* of church conversions—although one might contend that a public confession of racial sins, written or otherwise, is itself a central component in the ritual conversion of the racially born-again white southerner. The racial conversion narrative certainly follows what Owen C. Watkins has described as "the normal pattern" of Puritan conversion—"peace, disturbance, and then peace again." Indeed, narratives of racial transformation in the South during the past several decades have been what conversion narratives were to the Puritans—what Charles Lloyd Cohen has called "a psycho-cultural [phenomenon]."[6]

Conversion narratives, in a southern racial context, are also, as Patricia Caldwell writes of the Puritan narrative, a "literary phenomenon." James Cox has related the autobiographical narrative of the slave Frederick Douglass to Christian conversion narrative.[7] I would agree and go further—or, rather, reverse the assumption—and contend that the white racial conversion narratives of Lillian Smith, Lumpkin, Dabbs, Watters, and others are also, in their ways, "slave narratives," which is to say, also freedom narratives. That is, these writers too escape a kind of bondage, flee from the slavery of a closed society, of racial prejudice and restriction, into the liberty of free association, free expression, brotherhood, sisterhood—and freedom from racial guilt.

In this study I am interested almost exclusively in nonfiction, although any treatment of southern racial conversion could certainly include fiction

6. Owen C. Watkins, quoted by Caldwell, *Puritan Conversion Narrative,* 9; and Cohen, *God's Caress,* 160, n. 77.

7. Caldwell, quoted by Cohen, *God's Caress,* 160, n. 77; and James M. Cox, "Between Defiance and Defense: Owning Up to the South," in J. Bill Berry, ed., *Located Lives: Place and Idea in Southern Autobiography* (Athens, Ga., 1990), 121.

as well. Indeed, one might take as a kind of ur-text William Faulkner's "The Bear," whose protagonist, Isaac McCaslin, obsessed with the "cursed" South and desiring "peace" from ancestral racial guilt, serves virtually as a fictional prototype of some of these race-burdened southerners—just as fully as another Faulkner character, Quentin Compson in *Absalom, Absalom!,* is a prototype of those southerners such as W. J. Cash with a rage to understand and explain the South. Even better, and earlier, if one hopes to place this study in any sort of southern literary context, one might consider that first and most eloquent of white racial conversion narratives, the *Adventures of Huckleberry Finn.* Mark Twain's novel is, of course, a conversion narrative *malgré lui,* told by a narrator/protagonist who never fully realizes that he *is* converted. Henry Nash Smith's description of the battle between Huck's deformed conscience and sound heart—indeed, the whole concept of conscience as Samuel Clemens views it—is surely operative here. Many of the writers I will treat experience precisely Huck's conflict between "heart" and "conscience"—conscience, of course, being that socially conditioned guide to right and wrong, that "correct" version of morality (though often dictated as much by manners as by morals) dispensed by church, school, and family. Several of these writers, like Huck, look back on a time when they did right although they thought they were doing wrong—and vice versa. The difference in these southerners is that they, unlike Huck, *are* able to distinguish racial right from wrong at the point they tell their stories. All of these narrators, thus, are in possession of a dual perspective: as they write, they are conscious racial converts, aware of having passed through the conversion process and become changed creatures; but, for the most part, they are writing *of* a time before the conversion and thus they place the center of consciousness in the mind of younger versions of themselves. But even at that earlier point, before a conscious conversion, they too had often decided, as Huck finally does, "All right, then, I'll *go* to hell."[8]

Their stories, then, are those of Huck if Huck had, say, gone to a consciousness-raising university or joined a liberal church or covered the Civil

8. William Faulkner, "The Bear," in *The Portable Faulkner,* ed. Malcolm Cowley (1946; rev. ed., New York, 1967), esp. 252–306; Henry Nash Smith, *Mark Twain: The Development of a Writer* (New York, 1972), 113–37; Mark Twain, *Adventures of Huckleberry Finn* (1885; reprint, New York, 1948), 200.

Rights Movement—if his conscience, and therefore his *idea* of right and wrong, had ever caught up with his sound heart. But most of these writers—Smith, Lumpkin, Dabbs, Morris, and so forth—were (as Huck says of Tom Sawyer) "well brung up." That is, they found themselves with Huck's sensibility but with Tom's advantage—or disadvantage—of being "sivilized," of absorbing, far more than Huck, the rights and wrongs of school and church and respectable family. Particularly church: all of my primary subjects grew up in churchgoing families, and in most cases their families took institutional religion seriously indeed.[9] The rituals of conversion—that is, *conventional* religious conversion, through the church—were part and parcel of their lives (for all except perhaps the Episcopalians among them). They knew the rousing hymns, the earnest pleadings of revival preachers, the solemn marches down the aisle to the altar. They remembered the form of religious conversion long after, in most cases, they had rejected its substance. And they also remembered the emotions, the longing that created a vacuum nothing else had ever quite filled. No matter what these southerners had become, the religious impulse was planted deep. So was the habit, in their inner lives, of living meaningfully and dramatically.

Religious conversion, of course, had been a central part of southern life since the religious revivals of the early nineteenth century, the time when evangelical fervor had supplanted the old Anglican decorum in most parts of the South, and certainly in the upcountry. That conversion experience,

9. As far as a denominational breakdown is concerned, three of my primary subjects grew up Methodist, two Episcopalian, one each Presbyterian and Baptist, and one (Larry L. King) a Fundamentalist of no specified description. Of the writers I treat more briefly, Methodists and Presbyterians seem to predominate, with Baptists again underrepresented given their population in the South. It may come as no surprise that I found no (nonfiction) racial conversion narratives written by southern Roman Catholics or Jews—in part, of course, because of a lack of numbers in the South, at least until recently, but also, I would venture, because Catholics and Jews in most parts of the South were themselves "outsiders" (and thus occasional targets of hate groups such as the Ku Klux Klan), and because the conversion impulse, as it has operated in evangelical Protestantism, was foreign to their traditions. In fact, Jews had reason to be suspicious of conversion of any sort since they themselves were often the targets of evangelizing Christians. See, for an excellent treatment of this subject, and of southern Jews and race, Eli N. Evans, *The Provincials: A Personal History of Jews in the South* (New York, 1973).

as Anne Loveland describes it in *Southern Evangelicals and the Social Order,* was not substantially different from the earlier Puritan experience. That is, conversion involved "a conviction of sinfulness leading to feelings of despair and resignation which then gave way to a lifting of the burden of guilt and a feeling of acceptance by God." The moment of conversion "was a time of overpowering emotions," often accompanied by weeping and, finally, "great happiness."[10] And, as in earlier New England if in a somewhat different manner, the conversion usually resulted in church membership.

Southern evangelical ministers, preparatory to conversion, focused largely on individual sins such as drunkenness, adultery, and impiety—sins committed against God, one's family, or oneself—rather than societal, especially racial, sins. Social ethics, thus, was not necessarily a part of religion. Such had not always been the case in the southern church; in the late eighteenth century and the first quarter of the nineteenth it was not unusual for southern evangelicals to question what they believed to be ills of southern society, including slavery. But by 1830, with the abolitionist crusade gaining momentum in the Northeast, southern clergymen, as other southerners, began to turn to a defense of slavery in every way possible, including claiming scriptural sanction for the South's peculiar institution. Jon Alexander speaks of a "significant divergence" in patterns of northern and southern conversion after 1825: "Where Evangelical conversion in the North tended to propel converts into social reform, in the South it tended to bring converts a feeling of contentment."[11] Generally speaking, the southern church was set on a racial course it would maintain for nearly a century and a half.

The extent to which white nineteenth-century southerners experienced racial guilt, of course, has been widely debated. There is no doubt that in the early years of the century, as in the last years of the preceding one, such guilt was certainly present in the South. Thomas Jefferson's remarks about slavery in his *Notes on the State of Virginia* are often viewed as a complaint

10. Anne C. Loveland, *Southern Evangelicals and the Social Order, 1800–1860* (Baton Rouge, 1980), 4, 12.

11. Jon Alexander, quoted in Samuel S. Hill, Jr., *The South and the North in American Religion* (Athens, Ga., 1980), 71, 73. However, as Anne Loveland points out (*Southern Evangelicals,* ix), southern evangelicals did speak out about certain social ills—just not racial ones.

that *white* society was degraded by slavery: "There must doubtless be an unhappy influence on the manners of our people produced by the existence of slavery among us. . . . Our children see [the behavior of slave and master] and learn to imitate it." Such an interpretation of Jefferson's views is certainly correct as far as it goes. But more than self-interest was at work in his recognition of the "miserable condition" of the slave—a condition "in which he must lock up the faculties of his nature"—and even more so in his statement, "Indeed, I tremble for my country when I reflect that God is just: that his justice cannot sleep forever. . . ." Jefferson did regard slavery as morally wrong, and Jefferson, the slaveholder who did not free his slaves, certainly experienced guilt over the institution of slavery and his own participation in it. So did a number of other earlier southerners, particularly the clergy, and most particularly abolitionists such as George Bourne of Virginia, whose 1816 work *The Book and Slavery Irreconcilable*—"the most radical abolitionist tract yet to appear in the United States," according to David Brion Davis—stated flatly that slavery was sin. Several other southerners in the following decades, particularly Samuel Janney of Virginia and Daniel Goodloe and Benjamin Hedrick of North Carolina, opposed slavery on moral grounds. So did Mary Chesnut of South Carolina, although her concern was as much for the sexual temptation slave women presented for slaveholders as it was for the slaves themselves. Kate Stone of Louisiana felt a deeper personal burden. "Always, I felt the moral guilt of [slavery]," she wrote in her journal, "felt how impossible it must be for an owner of slaves to win his way into Heaven."[12]

Certain of the above concerns were voiced in the two decades preceding the Civil War, but in general by that time southern expressions of opposition to slavery had become rare indeed. After the New England abolitionists went on the offensive in the 1830s, the South was not about to indict itself. As we have seen, however, in a *personal* sphere, even after 1830, guilt was certainly no stranger to the South. In fact, in a private sense, it took an even stronger hold on the southern mind as the influence of the Scots-Irish, those rigid Presbyterians often called "Southern Puritans," became more

12. Thomas Jefferson, *Notes on the State of Virginia,* ed. William Peden (1787; reprint, New York, 1972), 162, 163; David Brion Davis, *The Problem of Slavery in the Age of Revolution, 1770–1823* (Ithaca, 1975), 200; and Kate Stone, quoted by Anne Firor Scott, *The Southern Lady from Pedestal to Politics* (Chicago, 1970), 50.

widespread. But, even more than before, religion and morality had little to do with slavery; as one Virginian, an evangelical minister, later wrote, looking back at antebellum days, "Whether slavery was right or wrong, was a question which I did not consider." As Samuel Hill has written of the relationship between personal and social guilt among antebellum white southerners, the recognition of forgiveness and salvation—gained by the church member through conversion—"enabled him to ignore his society's complicity in discriminating between races because he could relegate moral questions to the periphery." Ironically, "many southern whites got relief from the guilt of perpetuating an immoral socio-economic system by subscribing to the tenets of a guilt-oriented theology." Or as James McBride Dabbs has written, "The more guilt [the evangelical white southerner] felt for his private sins, the less he felt for his public, though all the time it was the existence of slavery . . . that furnished [an] unconscious guilt that spilled over into conscious guilt for personal sins." Focusing on the personal seemed to make the social simply irrelevant to one's obligations as a Christian. Indeed, as Frederick Douglass noted, among the harshest slaveholders were those who had found religion.[13]

But for all the discussion of the South's unconscious guilt, its repressed guilt, its defense mechanisms, and so forth—by Hill, Dabbs, W. J. Cash, and numerous other southern commentators—I would submit that many southern slaveholders, unquestioning souls as most people in any time and place tend to be, felt little or no guilt at any level over slavery. Rather, perhaps—in some cases—they experienced guilt over the *treatment* of slaves, but not the institution itself. After all, slavery had long coexisted, in some fashion, with Christianity; and southern preachers, as well as politicians, editors, and teachers, told white southerners that the scriptures sanctioned slavery. In fact, many of their leaders, though not usually clergymen, proclaimed the "positive good" defense of slavery, which held that white Europeans had done Africans a great service by bringing them to America and exposing them to Christianity.

13. Jeremiah Jeter, quoted by Loveland, *Southern Evangelicals,* 186; Samuel S. Hill, Jr., "The South's Two Cultures," in Hill, et al., *Religion and the Solid South* (Nashville, 1972), 41; James McBride Dabbs, *Who Speaks for the South?* (New York, 1964), 225–26; and Frederick Douglass, *Narrative of the Life of Frederick Douglass* (1845; reprint, New York, 1982), 117.

Indeed, for the white southerner, where social issues were involved—as in public life generally—*shame* was more likely than guilt to be operative, guilt being, at least in the realm of social issues, more of a New England commodity than a southern one. The distinction between shame and guilt—the one externally imposed, the other seemingly private and inner-directed—is not quite so great as it might at first appear, since, as again *Huckleberry Finn* teaches, guilt too can be externally imposed; that is, can be a conditioned response. Having said that, I would still by and large agree with Bertram Wyatt-Brown that "guilt is a more internal and self-dependent mechanism than shame,"[14] and would contend that the Old South, which valued honor more than conscience, would also thus place a higher value on shame (which was, after all, the absence—or, more accurately, the violation—of honor) than it would on guilt. Certain other elements of the nineteenth-century southern mind—the streak of Stoicism in many upper-class southerners, as well as the importance of manners (as more important than morals) in southern life—also lent themselves to a society that gave a higher priority to shame (that is, violating codes of manners, or losing face) than to guilt.

The Civil War did little to change that hierarchy. Never had the South seemed so haunted by God as in the years just after Appomattox, and it is true that certain southerners, particularly such divines as the staunch Calvinist Robert Lewis Dabney of Virginia, saw defeat as evidence of God's judgment on the South, and indeed experienced a kind of sectional guilt. But it was largely a guilt occasioned not by slavery but by what Dabney and others felt was southern impiety, materialism, and dissoluteness. When Cornelia McDonald of Virginia wrote of the South's "corrupt way," she had in mind primarily not chattel slavery but "money-loving, [the] courting [of] power, [and] striving for things which in all ages have been the ruin of nations."[15]

There were, to be sure, some few late-nineteenth-century southerners whose consciences troubled them over race. Atticus Haygood of Georgia, a Methodist minister, president of Emory College, and the son of a slave-

14. Bertram Wyatt-Brown, *Honor and Violence in the Old South* (New York, 1986), 52.
15. See Robert Lewis Dabney, *The New South* (Raleigh, 1883); and Cornelia McDonald, quoted in Dabbs, *Who Speaks for the South?*, 276.

owner, wrote *Our Brother in Black* (1881), which is as close as we come at
this time to a racial conversion narrative. Haygood had been moved to
write his book, according to Emory legend, after he had taken to task a
black janitor and had then felt great guilt for his action; he had prayed
about his racial attitudes, had asked himself (according to his friend, Methodist Bishop Warren A. Candler), "What would Christ do in my place?"
and had then proceeded to produce his book. "Time was," he wrote,
"when I did believe in [slavery] thoroughly, and when I defended it to the
last best of my ability." But "I have changed my opinions; rather, new and
purer light has changed them." For the most part, however, Haygood
would take a practical approach to race relations, and indeed he qualified
his criticism of slavery by holding to the old southern position that slavery
was "used by the mysterious but all-wise gracious providence of God to
prepare the negroes for their freedom."[16]

George W. Cable of Louisiana, often called "a Yankee Puritan" because
of his mother's New England stock and his own moralism, was one of few
other prominent southerners of the late nineteenth century who professed
anything resembling guilt over white racial sins. The son of a slaveholder
and himself a Civil War veteran whose southern loyalties were strong,
Cable was a reluctant critic, one who first gained recognition as a local-
color writer whose depiction of Louisiana life was charming and vivid. His
observation of southern racial injustice, however, prompted him to write
essays of social criticism in which he referred to the "moral evils" of slavery
and its aftermath, and in which he assured his audience that he wrote with
a "tone not of superior censure but of confession."[17] But as much as anything else, Cable, not given to personal revelation, used confession as strat-
egy—to assure his readers and listeners that he was one of them and possessed, or had possessed, the same racial prejudices.

In the final years of the century, as Jim Crow laws became entrenched
and Dixie moved deeper into its dark age of segregation, public expressions
of white racial guilt became rarer still. Even the few white social critics of
that period—figures such as Walter Hines Page of North Carolina and

16. Atticus Haygood, quoted by Joel Williamson, *The Crucible of Race* (New York,
1984), 90–91; and Haygood, *Our Brother in Black* (Nashville, 1881), 43, 44, 46.

17. George W. Cable, "My Politics," in *The Negro Question: A Selection of Writings on
Civil Rights in the South,* ed. Arlin Turner (New York, 1958), 19–20.

Lewis Harvie Blair of Virginia—approached race less on moral than on so-cial and economic grounds. Page, who found great success as a journalist and publisher in New York, spoke boldly about southern cultural and intel-lectual poverty but, in fact, rarely focused on race. He had his chance in a semi-autobiographical novel, *The Southerner* (1909), published anony-mously, but even here he held back. Blair, the Richmond merchant of high birth, spoke more boldly—in fact, his 1889 book, *The Prosperity of the South Dependent upon the Elevation of the Negro,* took the radical step of ad-vocating complete racial equality, including Negro suffrage and integrated schools, churches, theaters, and commercial establishments—but Blair quickly made it clear that he based his argument on "dollars and cents," not on "right, justice, morals, or religion." C. Vann Woodward believes that behind Blair's appeal to white southern self-interest lay a fierce moral indignation over racial injustice and a strong impulse of ethical reform. Per-haps that is true. And yet Blair had to frame his appeal altogether in terms of economics. And he later repented of his apostasy, leaving at his death in 1916 a 270-page undated manuscript, a sort of racial conversion narrative in reverse, in which he preached white supremacy, the Negro's "absolute subordination to the whites." He had returned to the southern fold.[18]

Such, at the very least, was the power at the turn of the century of the savage ideal, that condition, as W. J. Cash defined it, "whereunder dissent and variety are completely suppressed and men become, in all their atti-tudes, professions, and actions, virtual replicas of one another." Some few other white southerners—clerics Thomas U. Dudley, Quincy Ewing, and Andrew Sledd, as well as professor John Spencer Bassett of Trinity Col-lege—made mild protests against racial injustice, but their statements were rarely personal and never confessional. The same was true, two or three decades later, of Howard W. Odum, perhaps the most notable academic critic of the South during the first half of the twentieth century. As for the most prominent figures of the Southern Literary Renaissance, the *impulse* to address race in personal terms was certainly there—as part of that "auto-biographical impulse" Lewis P. Simpson has identified in southern writ-

18. Lewis Harvie Blair, quoted by C. Vann Woodward, in Woodward, Introduction to Blair, *A Southern Prophecy: The Prosperity of the South Dependent upon the Elevation of the Negro* (Boston, 1964), xxvi, xxvii, xlv.

ing—but not the desire, and perhaps not the courage, to confront race in personal and autobiographical, not to mention confessional, terms. Ellen Glasgow barely mentions race in her autobiography, *The Woman Within.* Faulkner assigns much of his guilt over slavery to the slightly ridiculous characters of Theophilus and Amodeus McCaslin, "Uncle Buck" and "Uncle Buddy" of "The Bear," as well as to Uncle Buck's son, the ineffectual Isaac, who indeed was burdened but for whom Faulkner—when asked at the University of Virginia—expressed little admiration or sympathy.[19]

The case of Allen Tate makes the point even more convincingly. In his brief essay "A Lost Traveller's Dream," an autobiographical fragment of some twenty pages, Tate brings to the surface material which should prompt racial guilt, particularly—as Lewis P. Simpson argues persuasively—his brief boyhood visit to an aged ex-slave of his family, a blood cousin by miscegenation. In his essay Tate also refers in passing to his lying about a petty theft he had committed as a boy, an act that led to the beating of a black friend. Tate could also have mentioned, but does not in this essay, coming upon the scene of a lynching when he was twelve years old. All this is powerful subject matter. A white southern writer born twenty years after Tate—indeed at least two or three writers, as we shall see, of Tate's own generation, less prominent and less tied to the southern literary establishment—would face such material directly, would trace its implications, would even use it as a springboard for a confession of personal or family racial sins. But Tate makes no such personal comment, other than to say of the betrayal of his friend, "I never made it up to him for my cowardice"—and to acknowledge, in a more general sense, that a complete autobiography "would demand more of myself than I know."[20] Tate would write

19. W. J. Cash, *The Mind of the South* (New York, 1941), 93–94; Lewis P. Simpson, "The Autobiographical Impulse in the South," in *Home Ground: Southern Autobiography,* ed. J. Bill Berry (Columbia, Mo., 1991), 63–84; and William Faulkner, cited in *Faulkner in the University,* ed. Joseph L. Blotner and Frederick L. Gwynn (Charlottesville, 1959), 245–46. For discussions of Dudley, Ewing, Sledd, Bassett, Page, W. P. Trent, and other southern self-critics at the turn of the century, see Charles Wynes, ed., *Forgotten Voices: Dissenting Southerners in an Age of Conformity* (Baton Rouge, 1967), and Bruce Clayton, *The Savage Ideal: Intolerance and Intellectual Leadership in the South, 1890–1914* (Baltimore, 1972).

20. Simpson, "The Autobiographical Impulse," 64–65, 71–73, 84; Walter Sullivan, "Strange Children: Caroline Gordon and Allen Tate," in Berry, ed., *Home Ground,* 124; and Allen Tate, "A Lost Traveller's Dream," *Memoirs and Opinions, 1926–1974* (Chicago, 1975), 7, 3.

a novel, *The Fathers,* in which he treated dramatically some of these elements of family and race, but he would never treat, in formal autobiography, self and race. Like the older Jefferson, who had lived in a society in which slavery had seemed to triumph, Tate preferred not to look into the abyss.

But if the canonical writers of the Southern Renascence, though possessing the autobiographical impulse, rarely addressed race autobiographically—as black southerners had done for three-quarters of a century—less prominent white writers, by the early 1940s, had begun to do just that. The outburst of white southern autobiography driven by racial guilt, beginning shortly before midcentury, would continue for three decades, indeed still continues to a great degree. If the autobiographical school of remembrance—reaching its apogee with the publication of William Alexander Percy's *Lanterns on the Levee* in 1941 and Ben Robertson's *Red Hills and Cotton* in 1942—had reigned up until then, the southern party of guilt seized control at about that time and has been preeminent ever since.

The phenomenon arose in the mid- and late 1940s from several factors: as a delayed response to the awakening of the southern critical spirit in the 1920s, which in the beginning assumed the form of the social criticism of Odum, Gerald W. Johnson, and W. J. Cash and which took the better part of two decades to assume autobiographical form; from the widespread travel and residence outside the South of most of the writers of autobiography within the southern party of guilt—among them Lillian Smith and Katharine Du Pre Lumpkin and James McBride Dabbs—an experience not unlike that of those southerners during and just after World War I who helped to usher in the southern *literary* awakening; from the social upheaval of the Great Depression and World War II; and, most of all, from the new realization immediately after World War II that the southern racial status quo could not last forever, that a racially integrated society, heretofore considered so remote in time as to be nearly inconceivable even by most southern liberals, was indeed possible and perhaps even at hand—a conviction that would grow increasingly stronger with President Truman's integration of the armed forces in 1948, the Supreme Court decision on school integration in 1954, and, especially, the beginnings of the Civil Rights Movement. To put it another way, what happened in the 1940s and 1950s to those white southerners who began to write books about race in personal, confessional terms is that the religious impulse—always there but, as it applied to race, long dormant—finally became operative. One might say, in fact, that in the 1940s, and more so in the following two decades, the great southern schism between religious impulse and social action, particularly concerning race— that division that had begun in the South in the 1820s, was nearly complete by the 1840s, and had lasted a full century—finally began to be bridged.

It was, in some measure, merely a delayed reflex, a response to the guilt that, as we have seen, had long been present at some level, indeed had accumulated over the years. If the postbellum North possessed, as Robert Penn Warren has written, a treasury of virtue, the white South contained a virtual reservoir of guilt, the floodgates to which were overdue to be opened. The southern writer of conscience was simply coming to assume what had been assumed in New England since the early nineteenth century—that the evangelical spirit which prompts personal salvation could just as certainly be put to the use of social, particularly racial, morality. Or, to put it another way, no true religious impulse can remain purely personal. As David Brion Davis has written, Jonathan Edwards and other seventeenth- and eighteenth-century Calvinists were the direct precursors of William Lloyd Garrison, Wendell Phillips, and other nineteenth-century New England abolitionists;[21] and just as surely as a line runs from the New England Calvinists to the abolitionists, so a line also runs, although less well acknowledged, from nineteenth-century southern Calvinists to twentieth-century moralists such as Lillian Smith and James McBride Dabbs. It is natural, then, to the latter-day southerner of Calvinist temper *and* a racially progressive bent that one's journey up from racism should be described in religious terms. If sometimes racism has been called a social problem, other times a disease (often, a "cancer" on the South), and still other times a "poison," most often it has been described by those writers who have examined it in very personal terms as, simply, "sin" or "evil." Those writers' penchant for giving voice to a litany of their own racial sins and thoughtless acts of cruelty might be seen as evidence that they subscribed, in some measure, to that old Puritan conviction that the greatest sinner was also the best candidate for salvation. Finally, despite the distaste for southern evangelists of one of the great-

---

21. Robert Penn Warren, *The Legacy of the Civil War: Meditations on the Centennial* (New York, 1961), 54, 59; and Davis, *The Problem of Slavery*, 296.

est of white racial saints, Lillian Smith, it is clear that she had learned from the evangelists of her childhood, that indeed she became a sort of evangelist herself. Just as surely as the revivalists of her early memory, Smith is saying "Repent and be saved!" The repentance merely assumes a different form. The South's vertical religion had at last become horizontal as well.

In every way the struggle with race on the part of the white writer of conscience was profoundly religious, and this became even more the case with the rise of the Civil Rights Movement. As Fannie Lou Hamer said to a group of black children who were about to integrate a Mississippi school, "They ain't gonna be savin' *you*. You gonna be savin' *them*." Or as Thurgood Marshall, less sanguine about the task, once remarked, "You know, sometimes I get awfully tired of trying to save the white man's soul."[22] But that was precisely, on one level, what the black southerner was called upon to do—an unfair burden, it might seem, given all the other burdens black southerners had to bear for white southerners. But white guilt was so deep, pervasive, and long-standing that *only* forgiveness by the oppressed could bring the oppressor—at least the conscious oppressor—inner peace. That desire, I believe, explains in part why several of the white southerners in the pages that follow felt so keenly and regretted so deeply the breakup of the spirit of interracial community—of blacks and whites together—in the latter days of the Civil Rights Movement. The movement had always been, for participating whites, in part about saving their own souls—about willing themselves back into a religion they could believe in—and their feelings of rejection within the movement in its latter days suggested they were not worthy after all.

In any event, the manner in which the regrets, fears, and desires of these committed white southerners—the newly converted, with a rage to tell their stories—would play themselves out at midcentury and beyond is the story I wish to tell. If the nineteenth-century white South, as Wyatt-Brown correctly maintains, was predominantly a culture of honor and shame, the mid-twentieth-century white South—or, rather, the white literary culture of mid- and late century, especially as it expressed itself through autobiography and very personal cultural commentary—was becoming increasingly a culture of racial guilt and repentance.

22. Fannie Lou Hamer, quoted in Willie Morris, *Yazoo: Integration in a Deep South Town* (New York, 1971), 21; and Thurgood Marshall, quoted in Harry S. Ashmore, *Hearts and Minds: The Anatomy of Racism from Roosevelt to Reagan* (New York, 1982), 495.

I

THE SINS OF THE FATHERS
Lillian Smith and Katharine Du Pre Lumpkin

IT IS NO ACCIDENT that the two southern writers who first emerged in the 1940s as authors of racial conversion narratives were women. It is no accident because what was, in most other respects, a liability for women—that is, a detachment from the centers of political, economic, and editorial power—was, in the area of social commentary and moral reflection, a distinct advantage. For the most part, women were restricted by no roles as official southern voices, bound by no firm institutional ties. From the time of Mary Chesnut, many women of position and privilege had functioned as a sort of Greek chorus, commenting—usually in diaries, journals, and letters—on the aspirations, triumphs, follies, and disasters of men, who, after all, controlled public affairs. "Placed, as plantation wives were, in close juxtaposition to slaves, responsible for their physical and spiritual well-being," Anne Firor Scott has written, "many southern women became secret abolitionists."[1] A tradition of dissent, extending back to the Grimké sisters of South Carolina, manifested itself in the early twentieth century in missionary societies, social action groups, and the antilynching movement. It is, in part, out of that tradition, a tradition with its origins largely in religion, that both Lillian Smith and Katharine Du Pre Lumpkin came. The spirit of that tradition gave them an advantage over their more prominent contemporaries, the reigning southern white liberals of their day, journalists Ralph McGill, Hodding Carter, Virginius Dabney, and Jonathan Daniels, all of

1. Anne Firor Scott, "Women, Religion, and Social Change," in Hill, et al., *Religion and the Solid South,* 93.

whom were very conscious of their roles as official southern spokesmen, leaders who believed they could not leave their followers too far behind. They were always careful—so careful that McGill, on the eve of the 1954 Supreme Court decision, still had serious doubts about desegregation of the public schools. Smith and Lumpkin had no such doubts.

"A modern, feminine counterpart of the ancient Hebrew prophets Amos, Hosea, Isaiah and Micah," McGill labeled Lillian Smith; a southern William Lloyd Garrison, Dabney said. Neither intended his description particularly as praise, yet each, in some measure, was correct. Smith was indeed prophet, crusader, one of the noncompromisers, the all-or-nothing southerners. Journalist Harry Ashmore once called her "an outright evangelist for the black cause," although I would add that, as she saw it, Smith's was also the "white cause," and that, even more than most evangelists, she was somewhat of the freelance variety, traveling from Atlanta to Charleston to Montgomery preaching the cause of civil rights—living life on the road while McGill, Dabney, Daniels, and Carter manned the equivalent of comfortable uptown pulpits in Atlanta, Richmond, Raleigh, and Greenville. The religious impulse had been present in Smith from an early age; at the Methodist revivals of her youth she had envied those who gave into religious conversion—"I remember how impossible it was for me to feel 'saved' "—and later she experienced her own form of conversion in her awakening to human rights. She wrote her narrative of conversion, *Killers of the Dream,* she later said, "in a way [as] an act of penance. . . . It was also for me . . . a step toward redemption." Once racially saved, as a good evangelist does, she sought to save others. As Scott Romine has written of *Killers of the Dream,* "Smith's narrative persona is evangelical in a cultural sense, attempting to invoke the culturally conditioned concept of religious sin within a social context. In constructing a narrative persona with such evangelical overtones, Smith assumes the voice of one who can tell the white South what it cannot tell itself as a means of effecting a cultural rebirth and salvation." Or, as Smith herself later said, she longed to create a "Christian democratic culture" in the South.[2]

2. Ralph McGill, "A Matter of Change," *New York Times Book Review,* 13 February 1955, p. 7; Virginius Dabney, quoted in Morton Philip Sosna, "In Search of the Silent South: White Southern Racial Liberalism, 1920–1950" (Ph.D. diss., University of Wisconsin, 1973), 309; Ashmore, *Hearts and Minds,* 96; Lillian Smith, *Killers of the Dream* (1949;

As a southern voice, Smith found herself even more marginalized than most women. Although her early life seemed conventional enough—she was born in 1897 in the north Florida town of Jasper, the seventh child of a prosperous businessman and his well-born wife—by her late teens she was set on a course different from that of most southern women. After moving, in her teens, with her family to their summer home in the north Georgia mountains, a move made necessary by her father's financial setbacks, she left for the Peabody Conservatory in Baltimore, where she studied music for four years, and then sailed for China, where she taught music in a mission school for the next three years. The stay in China had upon her the same effect that travel and residence outside the American South had for other southerners of her generation, and perhaps to an even greater degree: she came to see the South with new, critical eyes, and she became consciously detached from it as she had not been before. In the manner in which white Westerners dominated the Chinese, Smith saw reflections of what she had left behind.

When she returned to the United States, Smith remained an outsider in many ways. Though she was to achieve popular and financial success as a writer—largely for her best-selling novel *Strange Fruit* (1944), a sensational story of interracial romance and violence—she always felt unappreciated as a novelist. She wrote, later in her life, of being "curiously smothered": "When Southern writers are discussed, I am never mentioned; when women writers are mentioned, I am not among them."[3] She was correct in her assessment: at that time a number of more conservative southern women—Caroline Gordon, Katherine Anne Porter, Eudora Welty, and Flannery O'Connor to name a few—had been admitted to the southern canon. Lillian Smith had not been. She was rejected both by southern conservatives, particularly the Nashville Agrarians and their spiritual descendants, and by leading southern liberals such as McGill. During periods of her life she seemed less Isaiah or Micah—as McGill termed her—than Job. Twice her house burned—once by arson—and many of her papers and

---

rev. ed., New York, 1961), 93; Scott Romine, "Framing Southern Rhetoric: Lillian Smith's Narrative Persona in *Killers of the Dream*," *South Atlantic Review*, LIX (May 1994), 107; and Smith, "Autobiography as a Dialogue Between King and Corpse," in Smith, *The Winner Names the Age*, ed. Michelle Cliff (New York, 1978), 197.

    3. Smith, *The Winner Names the Age*, 217–18.

manuscripts were destroyed. In 1953 she learned she had cancer, and she was to spend the remaining thirteen years of her life battling its ravages, thus producing all of her later work in various degrees of pain and under a virtual death sentence.

It is little wonder that Smith sometimes felt alienated from much of the world around her, particularly the world of her native South. And there was one other reason for her alienation, one that she never acknowledged publicly but which in recent years Smith scholars, Rose Gladney in particular, have identified. Smith was a lesbian in a homophobic America—more to the point, in a homophobic South in which gender roles were more clearly defined, and the cults of manhood and womanhood held more sacred, than the rest of the United States. Lillian Smith was as bold an advocate of racial equality as the white South could boast, but she was not bold enough to deal publicly—in print—with her sexual orientation. She would create lesbian characters in her fiction, but she would not address the matter autobiographically. One might contend that her reluctance was a product of her Victorian upbringing, that one simply did not speak of sexual matters—although, in fact, Smith did speak openly and perceptively of sexuality in general, particularly the manner in which issues of sexuality intersected with issues of race. But to announce oneself a lesbian in the America of the 1930s and 1940s would be to violate an even greater taboo than racial integration. Indeed, concerning matters of gender in a broader sense, as her biographer Anne Loveland has written, Smith did not even identify herself as a feminist; she had been "embarrassed by the strident zeal of the women's rights advocates" of the 1920s.[4] And this from a woman who, as we shall see, recognized more clearly than any other southerner of her generation the destructive consequences of inflexible, enforced gender roles, who felt most keenly the subjugation of southern women.

4. Margaret Rose Gladney, Preface to *How Am I To Be Heard?: Letters of Lillian Smith,* ed. Gladney (Chapel Hill, 1993), esp. xvi; and Anne C. Loveland, *Lillian Smith: A Southerner Confronting the South* (Baton Rouge, 1986), 190. Smith's only reference to lesbianism in *Killers of the Dream* comes in a discussion of the southern suspicion of the arts and of artists, and that reference comes only in the 1961 edition: "The few who dared mess around in public with paints were usually looked upon as 'abnormal'—effeminate if men, lesbian if women" (188). In the 1949 edition the sentence reads "effeminate if men, masculine if women" (216).

On the subject of Smith's lesbianism, I would submit that her sexual identity was a major factor—just how major she herself perhaps did not fully recognize—in the making of Smith as a bold *racial* commentator. If she could not speak openly and personally on the one taboo subject, homosexuality, she would speak all the more boldly on another, racial integration. Her double detachment from the centers of southern power—not only as a woman but also as a lesbian—contributed to a perspective that allowed her to feel, in a manner white male heterosexual liberals never could, the pain of prejudice of any kind. McGill and Carter could feel sympathy for the plight of black southerners; Smith could *identify* with black southerners. She, too, was a pariah, was in some regard even more alienated than the black southerner because she could not even announce the reason for her alienation. Hers, in the well-ordered world of midcentury America, was a form of invisibility that, in one measure, was more socially destructive than that created by race.

But Smith would say—did say in broad terms— that barriers of race, gender, and sexual orientation, indeed any division or category that contributed to prejudices of any sort, were all part of the same problem. The great purpose of all her work was to demolish walls, barriers, between people—and racism and sexism as well as distinctions of class and religion built those walls. Her crusade against racism, then, was really a part of a larger crusade, against needless separation of any kind. The overriding theme of her work was a struggle against fragmentation, for wholeness. "My literary aim," she wrote an acquaintance in 1964, "has been to search and probe for the meaning of racism as a symptom of men's fear of the future, a symptom, too, of their fear of evolving into a more complex thinking human being." She often spoke of symptoms and symbols: the South itself, with its racial hatreds and fears, was "a symbol of something that must never be again." Finally, she maintained, as several of her fellow racial converts did, that "race prejudice and the fear of the unconscious, the fear of the depths of human nature . . . are harming the white people far more than the black people of the world. And the whites are going to do the most suffering before it is all over. But race is to me a symptom and a symbol of the white man's struggle with his own nature, his own God, his own world."[5]

5. Lillian Smith, letter to Phyllis L. Meras, 2 October 1964, in Gladney, ed., *How Am I To Be Heard?*, 310; Smith, in *New York Herald Tribune,* quoted by Will Brantley, *Feminine*

Smith originally entitled her first novel "Walls"—a book, never published, based on her China experience—but "Walls" could also have served as the title of her most notable book, *Killers of the Dream,* her narrative of confession (for her family and region as well as for herself) and of conversion. Originally published in 1949, and issued in a revised edition in 1961, *Killers of the Dream* was an impassioned plea for racial harmony as well as a harsh depiction of southern life, "a schizophrenic invention without parallel," one reviewer wrote, "an insane dichotomy from the cradle to the grave." Smith herself said her book could have been produced only "in a tight, closed culture": "A German, reared as a child in the Nazi days," might have written it. But she had written the book, she insisted, not to expose the South so much as to understand it—and herself. Her intent, "as was [that in] *St. Augustine's Confessions,*" she explained, was "not to give answers but to find the big questions that I could and must live with in freedom." Indeed, her book was "a kind of existential confession: this is life in a segregated culture as I saw it, felt it, heard it, experienced it, and was shaped by it." Or, as she commented another time, "I had to write this book. It was like a ghost flitting in and out of my mind until I did." She "had to find out what life in a segregated culture" had done to her: "I had to put down on paper these experiences so that I could see their meaning for me."[6]

Killers of the Dream had been a long time in the making; much of what Smith had thought and written over the previous fifteen years prepared her for it. In 1936 she and her longtime companion, Paula Snelling, had begun a magazine, eventually called *South Today,* in which she had pondered the sins of white southerners. Repeatedly she had written of the "racial fear and hatred" among southerners, the "profound guilt for our treatment of the Negro," and "the rationalizations by which the white man eases his guilt." Her own culpability she had proclaimed as freely as the seventeenth-century Puritans had confessed their sinfulness, declaring in an editorial

---

Sense in Southern Memoir (Jackson, Miss., 1993), 50; and Smith, letter to Jerome Bick, 9 September 1961, in *How Am I To Be Heard?,* 280.

6. Vincent Sheean, review of *Killers of the Dream* in *New York Herald Tribune Books,* quoted on back cover of 1963 Anchor edition; Smith, "Autobiography as a Dialogue," in *The Winner Names the Age,* 197; Smith, letter to George Brockway, quoted by Loveland in *Lillian Smith,* 220; Smith, quoted in John K. Hutchens, "Lillian Smith," *New York Herald Tribune Books,* 30 October 1949, p. 2; and Smith, *Killers of the Dream* (1961 ed.), 3.

entitled "Act of Penance": "We in the South who feel so much shame are not without sin. . . . We can now perform the ancient rites of handwashing . . . but we shall not be free of guilt until we rid our region of inertia and ignorance and poverty." She was well aware of her evangelical tone, remarking in a letter in 1939, "We sound like missionaries with a powerful solemn purpose." As she went about the business of converting others, Smith was also intent upon transforming herself. Even the writing of her novel *Strange Fruit* in the early 1940s had been "therapy" that "removed a long amnesia about my hometown." Smith "wrote down some things I did not know were true until I saw them staring back at me on the page."[7]

By the late 1940s, as Anne Loveland has written, Smith had become increasingly optimistic concerning race, and she was not alone in that optimism; as John Egerton has demonstrated in his magisterial *Speak Now Against the Day,* other progressive southerners, encouraged by the triumph of democracy in World War II and buoyed by President Truman's order integrating the U.S. Armed Forces, also felt that a breakthrough in southern race relations might be at hand. But Smith thought the reigning southern liberals were not seizing the day. In 1944 she had accused Virginius Dabney, John Temple Graves, and other liberals of being "racial thumbsuckers" who regressed to childhood prejudices during the stressful time of war.[8] Her thinking had changed little by 1949. If any white southerner were going to speak openly and truthfully about race, if anyone were to confess the white South's racial sins, it would have to be Smith. To segregation she would say no in thunder.

Smith later said that in writing *Killers of the Dream* she explored "layers of [her] nature" she had never touched before, that "my beliefs changed as I wrote them down." *Killers,* thus, was not only a book about her racial conversion; the writing process was part *of* the conversion, part of the shed-

7. Lillian Smith and Paula Snelling, quoted in Helen White and Redding S. Sugg, Jr., eds., *From the Mountain: Selections from Pseudopodia, the North Georgia Review, and South Today* (Memphis, 1972), xii, 67, 11, 42, 106, 133; Smith, letter to George Reynolds, 7 August 1939, in Sosna, "In Search of the Silent South," 327; and Smith, letter to Maxwell Geismar, 1 January 1961, in *The Winner Names the Age,* 214.

8. Loveland, *Lillian Smith,* 95–97; John Egerton, *Speak Now Against the Day: The Generation Before the Civil Rights Movement in the South* (New York, 1994), esp. 513–17; and Smith, *The Winner Names the Age,* 37, 46, 48.

ding of old beliefs, the transformation. The rhetoric of religious conversion pervades Smith's book. Earlier she had considered for her title "Give Us Tears," taken from a prayer by an old black preacher who, she wrote, had "told God about white folks, about a way of death in the South," and had concluded his prayer, "Break their hearts, oh God . . . give them tears. Tears."⁹ She ultimately rejected the title, but she kept much of the evangelical tone. In *Killers of the Dream* she speaks of blindness and light, of compassion, love, and redemption. She urges repentance: "But time has run out . . ." Racial discrimination and acute poverty were not social problems to Smith; they were "evils," and she indicts southerners for not "letting these evils enter the region of 'right' and 'wrong.' " The South she describes is a kind of hell, complete with "TERRORS," the Ku Klux Klan, lynchings, and the "singsong voices of politicians who preached their demonic suggestions to us as if elected by Satan to do so."

I must take issue with those who contend that Smith, if a severe critic of the South in *Killers of the Dream,* balances her criticism by offering an equal portion of the South's pleasures and charms. In fact, the overriding impression of the South is one of darkness, in Smith's own words "a tortured fragment of Western culture."¹⁰ The South she describes is virtually a nightmare society, a culture nearly as dark as that portrayed by Hawthorne as he looked back at his harsh ancestral Puritan New England, with *its* fears and ghosts and demons. "Even its children know that the South is in trouble," Smith begins her first chapter. "No one has to tell them; no words said aloud. To them, it is a vague thing weaving in and out of their play, like a ghost haunting an old graveyard or whispers after the household sleeps. . . . There is a heavy burden on all of us and as heavy a refusal to confess it" (15).

"This haunted childhood belongs to every southerner," Smith insists (15), and she considers the ways in which it is haunted. She remembers, as a child, "the bitterness on faces of my father's and grandfather's friends and other men on Main Street" (131), men "who clung to their white culture

9. Smith, *Killers of the Dream* (1961 ed.), 3, 7, 184, 2; and Smith, fundraising letter written on behalf of Americans for Democratic Action, 23 March 1949, in *How Am I To Be Heard?,* 124–25.

10. Smith, *Killers of the Dream* (1949, ed.), 223. The 1949 ed. hereafter cited by page number in the text.

as a cripple clings to his crutches; whose passion and memories had been deeply repressed, and who had put up signs long ago in their unconscious and had forbidden themselves ever to trespass them" (133). She remembers "the church and the home [that] kept guilt and hate" alive (118), the "ghosts who have haunted the southern soul too long" (119), the "terrifying sense of impending disaster [that] hung over most of us" (87). "From the day I was born," Smith writes, "I began to learn my lessons. . . . I learned that it is possible to be a Christian and a white southerner simultaneously; to be a gentlewoman and an arrogant callous creature in the same moment; to pray at night and ride a Jim Crow car the next morning and to feel comfortable in doing both" (19–20). She learned that no well-bred southerner would "call a Negro 'mister' or invite him into the living room or eat with him or sit by him in public places" (19). She learned that she was "better than a Negro" and "that a terrifying disaster would befall the South if ever I treated a Negro as my social equal" (18). And if she also learned that "to use the word 'nigger' was unpardonable and no well-bred southerner was quite so crude as to do so" (19), that lesson seems to have been as much a lesson in manners as in morals. Indeed, "one's mind and heart and conscience [were] blocked off from each other and from reality" (20).

Smith later maintained that her book, though a "personal memoir," was also "Every Southerner's memoir,"[11] and writing in 1949 she seems to assume that every white southerner feels as she does about the "haunted" past:

> We defend the sins and sorrows of three hundred years as if each sin had been committed by us alone and each sorrow had cut across our heart. . . . We have known guilt without understanding it. . . . We southerners have identified with the long sorrowful past on such deep levels of love and hate and guilt that we do not know how to break old bonds without pulling our lives down. (16)

Most white southerners lacked Smith's sensibility; they did not feel that they themselves had committed "each sin," that "each sorrow had cut across" their hearts, but Smith was nonetheless speaking for them in her act

---

11. Smith, *Killers of the Dream* (1961 ed.), 11.

of regional repentance. "Deep down in their hearts," she wrote, "southerners knew they were wrong. They knew it in slavery just as they later knew that sharecropping was wrong, and as they know today that segregation is wrong" (54); "always the South's conscience hurt" (62). It hurt as well because of the nearly five thousand lynchings in the eighty years since the Civil War; that was "a heavy sin for a democratic Christian people to live with" (62).

If Smith's repentance is for her region in general, it is for her family in particular. Both her father's and mother's families had been slaveholders, and, she later wrote, they had been "frank to admit that slaving is wrong, never defending it"—but they had also made "the most of it, a pretty penny off it, while it lasted."[12] In *Killers of the Dream,* however, she is more concerned with the sins of her immediate family:

> The Mother who taught me what I know of tenderness and love and compassion taught me also the bleak rituals of keeping Negroes in their place. The father who rebuked me for an air of superiority toward schoolmates from the mill and rounded out his rebuke by gravely reminding me that "all men are brothers," trained me in the steel-rigid decorums I must demand of every colored male. They who so gravely taught me to split my body from my feelings and both from my "soul," taught me also to split my conscience from my acts and Christianity from southern tradition. (17–18)

Smith vividly recalls the deformed conscience of her childhood, reflecting on such practices as shouting racial insults at black children and pushing them off the sidewalk. She realizes that such pastimes were not seen as "sins" at the time: "You do not have to pray about it, for it has never been mentioned in church or Sunday school. You know you will not go to hell if you push little colored kids into sandspurs . . . though you may go there if you steal a nickel. . . . Now, if you were to go to church or to school with colored children, that would be worse than a sin, worse than anything you know of" (86). As a child, then, Smith had felt no guilt for what she would later call racial sins, but "when we as small children crept over the race line

12. Lillian Smith, *The Journey* (New York, 1954), 61. Hereafter cited by page number in the text.

and ate and played with Negroes or broke other segregation customs that were known to us, we felt the same . . . overwhelming guilt that was ours when we crept over the sex line and played with our body" (78).

The finest example in Smith's book of her own Huck-like struggle between deformed conscience and sound heart—as well as the experience that, as she writes, "pushed [open] the doors" of her closed society "a little"—comes with her parents' apparent kindness to a child found living with a black family in a shack in the black part of town. Since the child appears to be white, she is taken from the black family, "despite their tears," and is brought into the Smith home. "She roomed with me," Smith writes, "sat next to me at the table . . . she wore my clothes, played with my dolls and followed me around from morning to night. . . . As time passed a quick, childish, and deeply felt bond grew up between us" (26–27). After three weeks, however, the Smiths discover the girl had come from "a colored orphanage," and Lillian is told that the next morning the child "would return to Colored Town." When Lillian asks why, her mother tells her the visitor is, in fact, "a little colored girl" (27). When Lillian protests, her mother grows visibly upset: "You're too young to understand. And don't ask me again, ever again, about this!" As the older Smith looks back, she tries to make sense of the incident: "I knew . . . that something was wrong. I knew my father and mother whom I passionately admired had betrayed something which they held dear. And I was shamed by their failure and frightened, for I felt that they were no longer as powerful as I had thought" (28–29). But young Lillian had "felt compelled to believe they were right. It was the only way my world could be held together. And, like a slow poison, it began to seep through me: *I was white. She was colored. We must not be together. It was bad to be together.*" Smith had felt "suddenly full of guilt": "For three weeks I had done things that white children are not supposed to do. And now I knew these things had been wrong." When the little girl, before she left, "crept closer and put her arms around me . . . I shrank away as if my body had been uncovered" (29–30).

The incident is revealing in a number of ways. At first, of course, it suggests the extent to which race is an abstraction: if one could not tell the "colored girl" was "colored" until she was labeled so, what difference should it make? But the episode shows as well the complicated nature of guilt, its operation on at least two levels. Just after her playmate left the

Smith home, Lillian felt guilty because, as a white girl, she realizes that she should not have been so close to a black girl—although, curiously, if the time and place had been different, say a southern plantation fifty years before (or, indeed, in Smith's own time), such closeness would not have been unusual, *if* racial roles had been clear from the beginning.

But roles had not been defined, lines had been crossed, and the adult Smith writes that young Lillian had experienced guilt for transgressing racial boundaries—although what she had experienced was more nearly shame than guilt. Later—at the time the mature Smith is writing—she feels an altogether different kind of guilt: she realizes how much she had hurt the "colored" girl, how she had violated what was natural and spontaneous because of the imperative of race. As is the case for Mark Twain's Huck, what she thinks is right is wrong, and what she believes wrong is right. But, unlike Huck's, Smith's deformed conscience wins—for the present. In the long run, however, the experience serves an important role in Smith's racial awakening. She comes to see that something is wrong with a world "that tells you that love is good and people are important and then forces you to deny love and to humiliate people. I knew, though I would not for years confess it aloud" (30). *Killers of the Dream,* of course, becomes that confession.

Looking back, Smith does not hold her parents primarily responsible for her own racial blindness; they, after all, were victims as well. She is less forgiving of the southern church, for its support of southern institutions (particularly racism), for its hypocrisy, and especially for its emphasis on the wrong kind of guilt: "Nowhere else, perhaps, have the rich seedbeds of Western homes found such a growing climate for guilt as is produced in the South by the combination of a warm moist evangelism and racial segregation" (95). Guilt, indeed, was "the biggest crop raised in Dixie, harvested each summer just before cotton is picked" (97), but that particular guilt, as in the older southern church, was occasioned by drunkenness, adultery, impiety, and other "personal" sins, not by racial transgressions.

Smith's attitude toward the evangelical church and its annual revivals is hardly simple. At the same time she finds religious revivals "a source of enormous terror," she also finds them "a blessed respite from rural monotony" (97). The evangelists, "in love with Sin" (99), fascinate her. The services themselves were "often prolonged for hours by those under conviction of sin who agonized and prayed and yet could not secure release from their guilt" (100–101). "Hymns, sermons on hell, invitations . . . to come to the altar and be saved, the dirgelike singing that embroidered our nerves, the revivalist's soft whispers and prayers when one finally broke down and went scuttling to kneel at the altar": this was "strong meat for children but we loved it" (102). Smith, however, was a reluctant convert:

> Though I went up to the altar and stayed until the revivalist pried me off my knees, I was never convinced that my kneeling had effected a change in either my present or future life. But sometimes, wanting it so badly, I lied and stood up with the rest when the evangelist asked all who were sure that they would go to heaven to arise and be counted. (105)

Then the evangelist sent "the town home vibrating with guilt and fear" (104).

The primary source of guilt in Smith's childhood, other than race, was sex. Indeed, the two were closely related in her mind. Though she takes issue with white southern stereotypes of blacks, she unwittingly reinforces that stereotype of African Americans as exotic primitives, "natural, vigorous, unashamed, full of laughter and song and dance, who, without awareness that sex is 'sin,' had reached genital maturity." Generalizing broadly, Smith insists that blacks had resisted the white puritan culture of the South, the "dark tangled forest full of sins and boredom and fears"; the Negro possessed, rather, a "physical grace and rhythm and a psychosexual vigor that must have made the white race by contrast seem a washed-out people, drained of much that is good and life-giving" (112). Smith was hardly the first southerner to see through the claims of white men who defended lynching on the grounds that it protected white women. Nor was she the first to suggest that a sort of sexual jealousy was at work: ". . . the lynched Negro becomes *not an object that must die* but a receptacle for every man's . . . forbidden sex feelings. . . . That, sometimes, the lynchers do cut off genitals of the lynched and divide them into bits to be distributed to participants as souvenirs is no more than a coda to this composition of hate and guilt and sex hunger and fear, created by our way of life in the South" (158–59).

White men were indeed the primary killers of Smith's southern dream of racial and sexual equality—it was quite literally the sins of the fathers about which she spoke—although her view of southern patriarchy, as for the other women in this study, is more complex than it might initially appear. First, although she is not altogether uncritical of him, Smith certainly loved and revered her own father; indeed, other southern daughters who wrote books in the late nineteenth and early twentieth centuries seemed, far more than Smith, virtually to worship their fathers. Such was the result of a number of factors—southern defeat in the Civil War, and thus the cult of the Lost Cause, which made heroes of many southern men, some deservedly, some not; the example of Robert E. Lee, wise, compassionate, the father figure *par excellence*; and the general influence of Victorian culture, which elevated the father to a position of often undeserved prominence.

Smith hardly succumbed to the same sort of father-worship expressed by other southern memoirists, but her respect for Calvin Smith was deep and abundant. She spoke of the southern woman's "curious loyalty to [her] own father, though every other man was not 'fit to be lived with' " (136). Even before she undertook *Killers of the Dream,* and in her work afterward, Smith saw the connection between racism and sexism in the South—as, indeed, numerous southern women had before her, particularly Mary Chesnut, who had written in her diary, "There is no slave, after all, like a wife." Elsewhere, Smith described men as creatures of design and abstraction, who possessed a "mass-lust for power" and warfare. Southern women, she maintained, had "never been as loyal to the ideology of race and segregation as have southern men." Indeed, woman had "smelled the death in the word *segregation*" because she herself had been segregated. Because of his "unending secret enmity against woman," man had placed her on a "pedestal . . . putting her always and forever in her 'place.' " Not only had southern women been an "oppressed group" whose minds "man put . . . in prison," but, worse, "we have grown to love our chains."[13]

Near the beginning of *Killers of the Dream,* Smith paints a brief but poignant portrait of her own mother, certainly a primary example of that woman who was subdued, controlled, and finally more than a little sad:

13. Mary Chesnut, diary entry of 9 May 1861, in *Mary Chesnut's Civil War,* ed. C. Vann Woodward (New Haven, 1981), 59; and Lillian Smith, "Man Born of Woman," in White and Sugg, *From the Mountain,* 240, 247, and "Autobiography as a Dialogue," in Smith's *The Winner Names the Age,* 191.

She was a wistful creature who loved beautiful things like lace and sunsets and flowers in a vague inarticulate way, and took good care of her children. We always knew this was not her world but one she accepted under duress. Her private world we rarely entered, although the shadow of it lay at times heavily on our hearts. (24)

Annie Smith was indeed one of that great "majority of southern women [who] convinced themselves that God had ordained that they be deprived of pleasure, and meekly stuffed their hollowness with piety" (137). The problem, Smith acknowledged, certainly went beyond the American South: "Who long ago made Mom and her sex 'inferior' and stripped her of her economic and political and sexual rights? . . . Man, born of woman, has found it a hard thing to forgive her for giving him birth" (151).

But, Smith adds, there existed a minority of southern women who, in the late nineteenth century, began to rebel against the patriarchy: they "went forth to commit treason against a southern tradition set up by men who had betrayed their mothers, sometimes themselves, and many of the South's children white and mixed, for three long centuries. It was truly a subversive affair" (140). Although white men were "unaware of it," the "insurrection was on" and "the old pedestal on which for so long their women had been safely stowed away was reeling and rocking" (141). Smith cites southern women who had led the crusade against lynching and thus "aroused the conscience of the South" and "tore a big piece of this evil out of southern tradition" (144). But she concedes that other southern women, like southern men, "found it easier to cultivate hate than love" (146).

Smith concluded the 1949 version of *Killers of the Dream* by indicting southern liberals—who substituted "paternalism for camaraderie" and were "confused by the word *equality*" (244)—and emphasizing the "power of love." The final chapter reaffirmed her contention that her book was about more than race; it was about psychological health in a larger sense. Throughout *Killers of the Dream* the language of psychology had competed with the language of religion; if racism was "evil," it was also "disease." Steeped in Freud, Smith spoke of "psychic fortifications," "childhood memories long repressed," and a "massive schizophrenic withdrawal" on the part of southern whites. There was much, she wrote, "that reminds one of mental illness in [the] catalogue of [southern] sins" (211). The psychoanalyst as well as the evangelist (the agendas of psychoanalysis and Puritanism had a great deal in common, Charles Lloyd Cohen has written), Smith rested her hopes in the ability of white southerners to overcome "our moral impotence" (255). To a black reader of *Killers of the Dream*—as, indeed, of most white racial conversion narratives—the author's thinking might have seemed somewhat self-indulgent. That is, attaining psychic wholeness for whites sometimes seemed for Smith to be at least as important as attaining equal rights for blacks. Was racial prejudice truly "harming the white people far more than the black people,"[14] as Smith asserted? A black southerner, still trapped in the nightmare of Jim Crow, would have had cause to doubt that.

When Smith reissued *Killers of the Dream* in 1961—with two new concluding chapters—she again preached the linked gospels of black rights and white psychological health. At this later date, the Civil Rights Movement gave her hope that both goals could be accomplished. She herself had suffered greatly since 1949, both from the cancer that had been diagnosed in 1953 (and she, more than any other memoirist, frequently described southern racism as a "cancer") and—equally painful to Smith—her continued rejection by the southern establishment, literary and otherwise. In 1954, shortly after she learned she had cancer, she had published *The Journey,* another very personal memoir, though one less about race than fear, hatred, and "walls" that "have almost smothered the goodness in us" (34). But racial sins—not so much Smith's as those of other southerners she encounters on a trip down the Carolina and Georgia coasts—and racial repentance were never far from her mind. She relates the story of a white motel owner, who seemed at first the epitome of kindness and generosity but whose racism, when it surfaced, "terrified" Smith, made her want "only to get away from this haunted place" (97). And she tells of another motel owner in Georgia who confesses to Smith his racial transgressions: "I asked [God] to forgive me for my sin. I saw it as plain as Saul of Tarsus saw his on the road to Damascus" (147).

In the mid- and late 1950s, in speeches and in essays, Smith continued to pursue the demon, segregation. In her 1955 treatise *Now Is the Time,* she

14. Cohen, *God's Caress,* 16; and Smith, letter to Jerome Bick, 9 September 1961, in *How Am I To Be Heard?,* 280.

hailed the 1954 Supreme Court decision—which, she maintained, had "freed whites"—and urged southern leaders to end segregation immediately; her words met with publicly respectful but condescending remarks from Ralph McGill, Hodding Carter, and Howard Odum. Racial segregation, she asserted, was "a symbol of the deep pervasive illness in our culture that has dehumanized us all"; it represented "that estrangement from God which oppresses modern man; it subsumes all the fragmentations of modern times." Racial guilt continued to be Smith's central theme: "To stem our guilt, we began to defend the indefensible: we declared that God had made the white race superior to other races." The emerging Civil Rights Movement in the late 1950s and early 1960s, however, gave her great hope: "By the reiteration of those powerful words *love, compassion, redemption, grace,* [it] is compelling us to search for truth, that of our region and of ourselves."[15]

Thus Smith brought to her expanded *Killers of the Dream* in 1961 a certain focused optimism she could not have possessed in 1949. She acknowledged that she had "changed" since she wrote the original version: "I am different. Because I wrote it."[16] In her new chapters she settled certain scores she had neglected to settle in 1949, in particular against the Southern Agrarians: "No writers in literary history have failed their region as completely as these did. . . . The tone was southern but if one listened carefully one could hear echoes of the post–World War One German thinking" (199–200). After remarking on affairs of the past decade and a half—particularly the American conflict with the Soviet Union and Communism (which Smith believed fully as dehumanizing as segregation) and U.S. relations with emerging nations in Africa and Asia—she again hailed the spirit of the Civil Rights Movement. The movement for Smith was far more than a crusade for black rights or even white "wholeness"; it was, in the truest sense, a spiritual experience, the coming together of God and racial concerns in the South for the first time in more than a century—the *right* kind

15. Ralph McGill, "A Matter of Change," 7; Hodding Carter, "Hope in the South," *Saturday Review,* 2 April 1955, p. 35; Howard W. Odum, letter to Guy Johnson, 20 June 1944, quoted in Sosna, "In Search of the Silent South," 347; Lillian Smith, *The Winner Names the Age,* 157, 158, 129, 62, 85; and Smith, *Now Is the Time* (New York, 1955), 36.

16. Smith, *Killers of the Dream* (1961 ed.), 3. The 1961 edition hereafter cited by page number in the text.

of religion for which her entire book had been a search. The philosophy of movement participants was "a mixture of Thoreau, Jefferson, Gandhi, Martin Buber, the teachings of Jesus and something uniquely theirs." And they were led by Martin Luther King, Jr., a "deeply religious young man with nerves of iron and emotions that lie down like lambs within him. . . . He is for the human being and he has taken his stand" (225).

Smith's concluding chapter in the 1961 *Killers of the Dream,* then, transcended race; it moved further and further into the realm of the spiritual, into a reflection on brokenness and healing and on man as a creature in a "dangerous state of flux," "only partially evolved" (212), and in need of redemption. Transcendence and redemption were again Smith's themes the following year in *Our Faces, Our Words,* also a tribute to the Civil Rights Movement and a work that is, in many ways, an extension of *Killers of the Dream.* After telling the stories of several civil rights workers and sympathizers—including a white minister, plagued by conscience, who has determined that "some of us whites may need to die for our collective sins"[17]— Smith speaks in the final chapter in her own voice. *"Redemption,"* she affirms, was the goal of the early Civil Rights Movement: "There was a surge of joy, of adventure, yes; of courage. . . . It was beautiful to see. Perhaps never in American history has there been a movement of such gayety and intellectual richness." Those associated with the movement were engaged in a "search for the good life which they hunger to substitute for the hollow thing-obsessed life too many of us have lived. And all of it streaked with a fine sense of humor and a humility they express in prayer" (122).

But that spirit was threatened, Smith insisted, by "intruders" in the movement, those who departed from nonviolence and embraced black nationalism, thus those who demonstrated that not all killers of her dream were white. She understood the reasons for the new militancy. "this intransigence of whites is now forcing a few desperate Negroes . . . in the nonviolent movement to try to take it over" (126). But it is *her* movement as well, Smith seems to be saying, and she resists such a takeover with all her waning strength. Her movement still envisions black and white together, is still "alive . . . growing . . . and is joyous, still a singing movement, still one full

17. Lillian Smith, *Our Faces, Our Words* (New York, 1964), 102. Hereafter cited by page number in the text.

of compassion and love" (127). And Smith did not want those who shared her philosophy of nonviolence to lose control to "those from the ghettos who have no hope, and who are too uninformed historically, too unsure emotionally to analyze current conditions or foresee the consequences of their acts" (128). If such words have the ring of white paternalism, Smith surely did not intend that; but it may be that even she, the most acutely sensitive of southern whites to the perils of paternalism, could not escape entirely that old assumption of whites that they knew what was best. Whose movement was it anyway? African Americans might have asked— *were* beginning to ask. Smith would maintain until the end that it was partly hers, that she wanted "compassion" and "love" and brotherhood to triumph.

Did she expect too much of the Civil Rights Movement? Had she made a religion of the movement in the same manner that earlier white southerners had made a civil religion of the Lost Cause, of white supremacy, of segregation? If she had, she was certainly not alone among white southerners of good will. In the years to follow, other heirs of the southern tradition, retaining the religious impulse but lacking the substance of the old faith, wrestling with their own racial guilt and seeking salvation where they could find it, would commit themselves, consciously or unconsciously, to a similar course.

Katharine Du Pre Lumpkin and Lillian Smith seem at first nearly parallel figures. Born within ten days of each other in December 1897, descended from Georgia planters and slaveholders, both grew up in families of position and privilege, dominated in each case by a strong father. In each case, financial circumstances required a family move—the Lumpkins, in Katharine's childhood, went from Georgia to South Carolina, as the Smiths had left north Florida to go back to Georgia. Katharine Lumpkin, like Smith, began to rebel against southern tradition in her late teens, and both women continued that rebellion in college—in Lumpkin's case, at Brenau, in north Georgia. Also like Smith, who left Georgia for Baltimore and then China, Lumpkin left Georgia at age twenty for Columbia University to study sociology and, after a period back in Georgia, for the University of Wisconsin, then perhaps the most progressive of American universities.

After two decades of teaching, research, and service in New England, during which she also produced books and articles on labor issues and became involved in social reform, Lumpkin in her late forties, like Smith, began to write her narrative of racial confession and conversion. Her memoir, *The Making of a Southerner,* appeared in her fiftieth year, just two years before Smith's *Killers of the Dream.* Personally, as well, the two would seem to have a great deal in common. Neither ever married; each lived most of her adult life with another woman, Smith with Paula Snelling, Lumpkin first with economist Dorothy Wolff Douglas and, much later, with Elizabeth Bennett—and Lumpkin, too, never wrote openly about her sexual orientation. Both Smith and Lumpkin in their writings and activities remained true to the tradition of southern women's activism, with its origins in Christianity, and each suffered for her unconventional beliefs. In some quarters Lumpkin, like Smith, was labeled a Communist; in this regard she suffered even more acutely than Smith. When a Smith College professor testified in 1953 before the House Committee on Un-American Activities that Lumpkin had belonged to a Communist Party faction within the American Federation of Teachers, Lumpkin found the experience shattering.[18]

Biographically and philosophically, then, Lumpkin and Smith indeed had a great deal in common. In the manner in which they went about the business of social change, however, they were vastly different. A Micah or an Isaiah, Lumpkin was not; she was not so combative as Smith (or, for that matter, as her own sister, Grace Lumpkin, a proletarian novelist), was less a public presence, less the evangelist, not given to traveling from place to place, preaching the gospel of equal rights. Their difference, then, was in part one of *tone,* and this may have come in some measure from their backgrounds. Both were strongly influenced by religion—Lumpkin's racial conversion, like Smith's, was described in quasi-religious terms—but Lumpkin's early religious training was quite different from Smith's. Although her

18. Jacquelyn Dowd Hall, biographical entry on Lumpkin, forthcoming in *American National Biography,* ed. John A. Garraty (New York). For biographical information (besides that contained in *The Making of a Southerner*) I rely primarily on this entry as well as Hall, "Open Secrets: Memory, Imagination, and the Refashioning of Southern Identity," *American Quarterly,* L (March 1998), 109–24, and Hall, " 'You Must Remember This': Autobiography as Social Critique," forthcoming in *The Journal of American History.*

father's family had been Baptist, her mother's was Episcopalian; and Katharine Lumpkin's immediate family, staunchly Episcopalian, distrusted the display of religious excess associated in their minds with Methodists, Baptists, and Presbyterians. Unlike Smith, who as a child embraced religious revivals, feeling regret only in her inability fully to heed the evangelist's call, Lumpkin—upon first attending a revival at age twelve—felt "many stirrings of embarrassment" for those "who had been converted, my schoolmates especially; it seemed so public somehow to my Episcopal soul."[19]

But conversion of another sort Lumpkin experienced just as surely as Smith did, and *The Making of a Southerner* is her story of that transformation. Written at a point just after World War II when she, like Smith, saw signs of racial change in the South, it was the most personal book Lumpkin would ever write, yet it was more subdued, less polemical, than *Killers of the Dream*. Lumpkin begins her story speaking as one of the southern status quo, and it is a voice she sustains for nearly half the narrative. Indeed, at first she speaks not so much as an individual but as a member of a family, and the events she describes in the first hundred pages, events from antebellum and Reconstruction days, occurred long before she was born. But so detailed is her description of her grandfather's 1,200-acre plantation in middle Georgia, so apparently sympathetic her depiction of plantation life, that if one did not know otherwise one might think she had actually experienced what she describes and that she approves of that life altogether.

It is, in every sense, the world of her fathers Lumpkin depicts, and it is from the point of view of the slaveholder, her grandfather, that she sees that world. She portrays her grandfather as a kind master of his more than fifty chattels, and she describes slavery, on his plantation at least, as a rather benign institution. We are shown a world of close loyalties between master and slave, a world of good spirits and good humor; the romantic description of Christmas, with kind masters giving gifts to grateful slaves, could have been taken from Thomas Nelson Page. "Of Bondage to Slavery" she titles her first chapter, the implication being that her grandfather is the one in bondage—that his slaves own him.

When the war came in 1861, Lumpkin's father was twelve years old; as

19. Katharine Du Pre Lumpkin, *The Making of a Southerner* (New York, 1947), 168. Hereafter cited by page number in the text.

the "young master," she writes, he commanded the respect and loyalty of the slaves over whom he believed he was destined to preside. And when, at age fifteen, he went off to fight, he took with him his body servant. The portrait of William Lumpkin returning from war could also be taken from the stories of Thomas Nelson Page: "So it was, on an evening in May 1865, Father came home from war. Beside him rode black Pete, his body servant, who had gone away with him and stayed by his side during his soldiering and now was returning, still by his side" (51). Her father had told Pete he was free to leave, but "of course Pete stayed": "Indeed, although Pete came and went as a free man, in the two decades that followed, he never really left the roof of his none too affluent former master nor broke the peculiar tie which their upbringing had forged" (74). "I cried when old Pete died," her father reported.

Such a depiction of the Old South makes for a curious beginning to a work of racial confession and conversion, and Lumpkin continues in the same vein in her description of Reconstruction, which she sees from the point of view of the landed white southerner, burdened and oppressed by freedmen, carpetbaggers, and scalawags. It is a curious beginning but, as the book develops, a most effective one. For in order to write of conversion Lumpkin must first describe what she was converted from, what she earlier believed. *The Making of a Southerner* is a triumph in point of view, a work in which the author very carefully employs a dual perspective—both that of the author, nearing fifty, having rejected altogether the South of hierarchy and racial segregation, and that of the young Katharine, who had fervently believed in just that earlier South. In the first half of the book she resists the temptation to violate the point of view of the child—which is also the point of view of her family. When she describes the slave quarters, or refers to slave auctions and the price of slaves, she is altogether nonjudgmental; and one finds virtually nothing in the early narrative to suggest that she, as she writes, has changed. There is certainly nothing of the moral censure of Lillian Smith.

But there is, if one reads closely, a certain undercutting of her *apparently* sympathetic portrait of her grandfather and the plantation. She writes that her grandfather did not believe in breaking up slave families, but then adds that "circumstances" could interfere and make him act otherwise (12). She writes that the "personal conduct" of her grandfather "in relation to [his] slaves" was "beyond reproach," and adds "as [he] saw it" (17). She reveals that her grandfather strictly obeyed the law and did not allow his slaves to learn to read—this at a time when some slaveowners did not adhere to that law.[20] She writes that her grandfather was "in no wise a harsh man" (29), yet adds, "True, according to Father, he felt as strongly as the next how firm an owner must be in requiring instant obedience. He was swift to curb any 'rebellious' spirit, and hold 'lazy' slaves to their tasks, lest they set demoralization loose in the quarters" (29). And she reports, in the near humorous tone in which the story had been reported to her, the frequent efforts of one slave, called "Runaway Dennis," to escape—without suggesting *why* he might have wanted to escape, although she knows that the reader, if the reader resembles Katharine Lumpkin as she writes in 1946, will surely consider the matter. In these ways and others Lumpkin has it both ways: she appears to be loyal to the traditional South, as the young Katharine would have been, but she also provides evidence (that the child would not have recognized as evidence) that all was not as idyllic as she has suggested. Somewhat like William Alexander Percy, writing of his father in *his* autobiography, *Lanterns on the Levee,* which had appeared only five years earlier, Lumpkin both pays homage to the world of her fathers and, in certain important respects, undermines that world at the same time.

Even more than with Lillian Smith, it was indeed the world of the *fathers* that mattered. Lumpkin, at least on the surface, nearly fits into that postbellum southern school of father-worship seen in such works as Susan Dabney Smedes' *Memorials of a Southern Planter* (1887). Lumpkin's father, she reports, had read law with Alexander Stephens after the war; he had become a favorite speaker for Confederate veterans gatherings; a representative of the old order, he had entered the primary race for the U.S. Senate in South Carolina in 1908, only to lose to the populist Cotton Ed Smith. Lumpkin speaks of her father's great reputation as "a teller of tales": "how profligate

---

20. Lumpkin writes of one slave, Jerry, who served as a preacher to the other slaves and who, although said to be illiterate, was reputed to have a phenomenal memory: on Sunday mornings Lumpkin's grandmother would read him a chapter in the Bible, and that afternoon, at the slave service, he would look at the Bible and quote the entire chapter. It later seemed "conceivable" to Lumpkin that Jerry had "worked a life-long deception on his master and mistress," that in fact he had been able to read the entire time (224). But as a child she had accepted the story as she heard it.

he was with his stories, how inexhaustible his store, how invariable his technique" (122). In his manners William Lumpkin was also "a goal and example": "Where other men were courteous, he made an art of courtesy. Who could show so much deference to a lady, and more than any other, to his wife? Who could bow from the hips with more formality and grace than Father?" (122).

William Lumpkin was also famed far and wide as a devotee of the Lost Cause. "Impregnating our lives with some of his sense of strong mission" (121), Lumpkin writes, he "baptized" his family, particularly Katharine, in the sentiments of the Lost Cause. Katharine's mother belonged to the United Daughters of the Confederacy, and Katharine herself—after having been "dipped deep in the fiery experience of Southern patriotism" at a Confederate reunion when she was five—joined the "Children of the Confederacy" (112). She absorbed as well her father's interpretation of southern history, his painful memories of Reconstruction: "These stories deeply affected him. He could still feel anger when he told us of them" (73). Her father, who had joined the Ku Klux Klan after the war, told young Katharine "of Negroes' 'insolence' and 'uppitiness.' . . . He felt that he must tell the story" (86). He spoke in particular of a black man who, he said, pushed him off the sidewalk and spat at him; he said his own mother was prevented from passing down the street by a Negro woman. And Katharine, as everyone else in her family, accepted his interpretation of events: "To my people, as to me in my childhood, who was reared in their history . . . no 'two sides' to what happened was conceivable" (87).

The Lost Cause, even more than Episcopalianism, became the true religion of the Lumpkins. "How the plaster walls of our parlor," Lumpkin recalls, "rang with tales of the South's sufferings, exhortations to uphold her honor, recitals of her humanitarian slave regime, denunciation of those who dared to doubt the black man's inferiority, and, ever and always, persuasive logic for her position of 'States Rights' " (125). "We must keep inviolate a way of life," Lumpkin was taught. "It was inconceivable . . . that any change could be allowed that altered the very present fact of the relation of superior white to inferior Negro. This we came to understand remained for us as it had been for our fathers, the very cornerstone of the South" (127–28). Thus, she continues:

> My ears were saturated with words and phrases . . . carrying a special
> urgency: "white supremacy," "Negro domination," "intermarriage"
> . . . "good darkey," "bad darkey," "keep them in their place." As time
> passed, I myself would learn to speak these words perhaps with special
> emphasis, given the times and tones of others' voices saying them,
> even before I had the understanding to grasp all they stood for. (130)

Such was the power of conditioning in the Lumpkin home, a home over
which William Lumpkin presided with almost dictatorial authority. Such
were the values Katharine Lumpkin was taught to hold sacred, values from
which she would later depart altogether. In all her remarks on her father in
The Making of a Southerner she never directly criticizes him, never openly
challenges his authority. He remains the epitome of the "Southern gentleman."

And yet, as with her undermining of her own portrait of the idyllic
world of the plantation, Lumpkin also undermines the paragon she has depicted her father to be. The *facts* she presents do not always support her
characterization. At certain points in the narrative one cannot be altogether
certain that she is not resorting to irony—or sarcasm—or at least deep resentment. It is tempting to see at least some irony in the following description of William Lumpkin by Katharine Lumpkin, feminist and racial iconoclast at the time she wrote in 1946: "Father, head and dominant figure,
leader, exemplar, final authority, beyond which was no higher court in family matters; one who, even outside our circle, plainly possessed prestige and
recognition for the role he played. . . . A unique man, in our eyes, perhaps
in others'" (121). Yet, knowing the penchant of enlightened southern
daughters for seeing through men in general but exempting their own
fathers, I cannot be sure this is irony—or resentment—after all.

What is much more telling is Lumpkin's description of an event in her
childhood that is, in many respects, her equivalent of Lillian Smith's childhood encounter with the little "white" girl who turns out to be "colored."
One day, in her parents' yard, Katharine hears from within the house "calls
and screams," and she knew "someone was getting a fearful beating":

> Carefully keeping my distance, I edged over so that I could gaze in
> through the kitchen window. I could see enough. Our little black
> cook, a woman small in stature though full grown, was receiving a se-

vere thrashing. I could see her writhing under the blows of a descending stick wielded by the white master of the house. I could see her face distorted with fear and agony and his with stern rage. . . . I could hear her screams. . . . Having seen and heard, I chose the better part of stuffing my fists in my ears and creeping away on trembling legs. (132)

"The thrashing of the cook was not talked about," Lumpkin writes, "not around me at least. Nothing was said in the family, although a strained atmosphere was present all day." When Lumpkin asks what the cook had done, "I was told simply that she had been very 'impudent' to her mistress; she had 'answered her back' " (132). Lumpkin adds, for once intruding on the point of view of the young Katharine, "It was not the custom for Southern white gentlemen to thrash their cooks, not by the early 1900's." But quickly retreating to the perspective of the child, she immediately explains, "But it was not heinous. We did not think so. It had once been right not so many years before. Apparently it still could be" (132).

The adult Lumpkin, the author, knows it had never been "right," but she will not violate the point of view of the child Katharine except for a moment. By choosing to relate the incident in the first place, however, she has already done more damage to her father than any analysis of the act might do. She has told a story that calls into question the portrait of her father she had taken such pains to paint—a southern gentleman of grace and manners, given to *noblesse oblige*. The beating of the cook has such an effect upon her that she cannot even bring herself to refer to the perpetrator of the beating as "Father." She must call him only the "white master of the house," and in the process she detaches herself from what has just occurred. The term "white master" is loaded, of course, since it connotes the earlier master of the southern plantation, and further connotes, in the sense that George Fitzhugh and other antebellum southerners had meant it, the master of an extended family, an entire domain, including wife, children, and slaves.

Lumpkin did not easily leave this episode behind. She tried to reason that the beating of the cook must have been justified because of the cook's "impudence." In that sense, "I had no qualms about what I had witnessed." But "in another sense I did have, and this disturbed me. Naturally

I had no explanation for these mixed feelings. I could merely try to forget the thing" (132–33). As with Lillian Smith, however, after her own painful childhood encounter with the realities of race, Lumpkin could not forget entirely: "Thereafter, I was fully aware of myself as a white, and of Negroes as Negroes. Thenceforth, I began to be self-conscious about the many signs and symbols of my race position that had been battering against my consciousness since virtual infancy" (133).

Lumpkin includes no further episodes that undermine the position of her father as exemplar and gentleman. But one later mention of him, by its very matter-of-factness, seems equally devastating. It occurs in that part of the narrative in which Lumpkin describes her family's move, when she was eleven, from the city of Columbia to a farm in Richland County. She reports that, upon arriving at the farm, her father hired help, decided which fields would go into cotton and which into corn, and prepared the soil for planting. Then she adds: "However, only three months after we reached our new home, Father, while away on a trip, was taken ill and a few days later died. For the time being we could but continue on the farm. One could not in a moment make satisfactory disposition of a place just purchased" (153). And that is all! After all her praise of her father, after speaking of her devotion to him and all he represented, this is all she has to say about her father's death. She makes no mention of her emotional reaction to his death, nor that of anyone else in her family. His death seems merely an economic inconvenience.

Whether such timing is important or not, his death comes just after that point in the book that Lumpkin has begun to write of her family's and her own racial sins—although she hardly recognized them as sins at the time. She recalls that she and a friend were "outraged" when a small black girl did not move off a sidewalk as they approached; the black girl's arm had brushed against Katharine's friend, who turned "furiously" on the girl and shouted, "Move over there, you dirty black nigger!" (134). Another time she and her friends began "a Ku Klux Klan," complete with sheets and hoods: "A chief topic of business . . . was the planning of pretended punitive expeditions against mythical recalcitrant Negroes. . . . We vented our feelings. We felt glow in us an indignant antagonism" (136). And she and her family "decried those who from within criticized lynchings." "The occurrence of lynchings was entirely understandable," she had reasoned, "the noble motive of outraged white males attempting to protect 'white Southern womanhood' " (179).

Lumpkin, as Lillian Smith in *Killers of the Dream*, brings a dual point of view to her discussion of sin: what is "sin" for the mature Lumpkin is not sin for young Katharine. In fact, it is precisely the opposite. Keeping her perspective altogether in the child's mind, Lumpkin writes, "Often we spoke of the sin it would be to eat with a Negro. Next to 'intermarriage' this was a most appalling thought. It was an unthinkable act of 'social equality.' . . . We were sure Yankee teachers in Southern Negro institutions were guilty of the sin." Similarly, when President Theodore Roosevelt entertained Booker T. Washington in the White House, "we were all aroused. . . . We children talked of it excitedly, echoing the harshly indignant words and tones" (135).

Although Lumpkin's deformed conscience, she suggests, remained intact concerning race until at least her mid-teens, her experiences at the farm contributed to her awakening, including her eventual racial awakening, in other ways—contributed, that is, to the breakdown of an inherited southern mythology of which white supremacy was a central part. First, the place her father had purchased was far from grand—a two-hundred-acre farm, nothing close to the plantation of family lore. Further, Lumpkin discovers, "it was in poor farming country," near the South Carolina Sand Hills (151); the soil wasn't even good. Up until this point a town and city girl, Lumpkin is awakened as well to the lives of the black laborers who work on the farm: "From whence, who knows, I had thought to see 'jolly black laborers' singing in the sun as they trudged along between the cotton rows. I had thought to hear jokes bandied back and forth, and see 'white teeth gleaming with happy grins.' . . . I had thought they would treat me . . . outgoingly, responding with hearty pleasure to my little attempts to be friendly" (155). But she sees none of that. The workers are polite but "remote," working "silently"; they are "somber strangers," "people carrying some kind of burden with which they were preoccupied" (156).

At her farm near the Sand Hills the young Katharine receives an education in class as well as race. She attends school with downtrodden whites and is struck by their grim lives—the clothes they wear, the food they eat, the way they talk. Since there is no Episcopal church for twelve miles, she goes to a rural Baptist church where she witnesses the workings of evangelical religion. Because Katharine and her brother like to dance, they are soon seen as outcasts in the little church and, finally, in the community as well: "Thus my last months in this sandy country ended in a sort of ignominious isolation from the people around us whom once I almost felt I had come to know" (173). She and her family soon return to the city, happy to be leaving the farm, but Lumpkin later sees the sojourn in the country as a turning point in her life:

> Something, it seems, was begun out there in the Sand Hills. Something apparently had been taken away, even if at the time I did not acknowledge it. For where was the full glamour now of the "old plantation," when in recent first-hand experience there was only a "farm," and this under circumstances of poor country, hard work, and people who seemed not to enjoy it at all? Why would not the old picture be blurred by the insertion of this new one, in which Negro laborers came and went as strangers . . . Negro laborers, moreover, who seemed borne down by extremities of destitution which I had never witnessed even for Negroes (182).

What Lumpkin had experienced was not just an education in race. What had happened, in a larger sense, was that the romanticism had fled and realism crept in. She does not make the connection, but it is interesting that the beginning of her education in the realities of southern life comes just after the death of her father—who is no longer around to counter any doubts she might have about the idyllic South. In any event, not only was her father dead, but—as concerns its powerful mythology—the world of the fathers as well. As she later wrote:

> Here in actuality was the moment when chance circumstance showed me our native Tree of Life, and had me eat of its revealing fruit. To all effects that act shut me out from my erstwhile Garden of Eden. For, once my eyes had been opened, it would seem, I never again could return to the comfortable ignorance which would have let me assume as an unfortunate inevitability the destitution, the drabness of life, the spiritual and material exploitation, which was the lot of so many. (239)

Lumpkin entitles the chapters coming just after her Sand Hills experience "Of a New Heaven" and "And a New Earth"—titles that capture the spirit of transformation she felt as she left home for college at Brenau, some fifty miles north of Atlanta. It is only when she discusses her college days that Lumpkin speaks of her mother at any length. Earlier she had said that Annette Lumpkin had "remembered with persistent vividness her pleasures on the plantation" (53) as a child; her mother, that is, seemed to have exactly the same view of the Old South and its charms as Katharine's father. Now, enrolled in college classes, Katharine realizes that she herself has read more widely than her classmates, has a "lively intellectual interest"—and that her mother "in particular had had a hand in it." We learn that her mother had always been a heavy reader, had realized as a child "the worth of her mind" (185), and had felt that young women were just as entitled to higher education as young men.

At Brenau, Lumpkin undergoes not only an intellectual awakening but a religious one as well. She becomes acquainted with the social gospel, an activist religion that "told youth that the day of discipleship was not past":

> On the contrary, it said that the essence of their religion did they but know it, was old words with a new meaning—"Follow the Master" . . . How, we began to wonder, . . . had men been so blind for all the generations of Christendom as not to see what we now perceived? . . . Why, our minds demanded, was there still so little "brotherhood" in the world, when "brotherhood" was the very meaning of Christianity? Let enough people but be persistent enough . . . and why might not the new day mankind hoped for begin to dawn? (188)

With Lumpkin, "brotherhood" comes to mean racial justice, but her steps in that direction are tentative; old prejudices are hard to overcome. She first confronts a "crossroads" when a leader at a YWCA conference proposes bringing in an African American woman, a Miss Arthur, to speak on Christianity and race. "Would we be introduced and have to shake her hand and say: '*Miss* Arthur'?" Lumpkin asks (189). She goes on to describe one of the major steps in her racial conversion, employing in this instance not the language of blindness and vision but (as she had in discussing her Sand Hills experience) that of original sin:

> We were like a little company of Eves, who, not from being tempted—surely, we did not long to eat the fruit which up to now

had been called forbidden—but by sheer force of unsought circum-
stance found ourselves called upon to pluck from the Tree of Life the
apple that would open our eyes to see what was good and evil. But
here the confusion reigned. We had been taught it was wrong to eat
this apple. Yet as it was put before us we felt guilty not to. (191)

"Why," Lumpkin asks, "did we consent?" Why did she violate the pre-
cepts "of a Lost Cause termed sacred" (191)? She did in part because, like
a sinner in a revival service, she felt she had virtually no choice. Just as the
evangelist uses the scriptures to persuade his potential converts to come
forth, so the YWCA leader used the story of the good Samaritan to persuade Lumpkin that, if she were to "follow the Master" (the *new* master,
not the earlier "white master"—her father), she must accept the black
speaker. What the speaker said, Lumpkin continues:

> was not of such great consequence: what mattered was that she en-
> tered the door and stood before us. We told each other afterwards . . .
> how our pulses had hammered, and how we could feel our hearts
> pound in our chests. Be that as it may, it was of no small moment to
> hear her low voice sound in the speech of an educated woman, and to
> have my mind let the thought flicker in, even if it disappeared again
> immediately—If I should close my eyes, would I know whether she
> was white or Negro?
>   In any event, when it was over, I found the heavens had not fallen,
> nor the earth parted asunder to swallow us up in this unheard of
> transgression. (192–93)

Lumpkin compares her awakening, finally, to the story in the book of
Samuel of the man who, violating sacred law, touched the Tabernacle of
Jehovah and was stricken dead. She too had touched "the tabernacle of our
sacred racial beliefs." How ingrained in her "were the beliefs it housed, and
the belief that to touch it would bring direst consequences." But "I had
touched it. I had reached out my hand for an instant and let my finger-tips
brush it. I had done it, and nothing, not the slightest thing had happened"
(193).
    After her racial conversion, Lumpkin is indeed transformed. When at
age twenty she goes to Columbia for graduate school, she finds herself in a

seminar with three African American women, one of them Georgia-born and assertive, and at the end of term they all attend a tea the professor gives. "It was not without full knowledge of what I was doing," Lumpkin writes. "This was 'eating with Negroes.' In the terminology I once had used this was 'social equality.' In the whole roster of Southern taboos it was nearly the most sacred. It was a grievous Southern sin for which were allowed no mitigating circumstances." Earlier in her life, Lumpkin adds, such a transgression "would have seemed a momentous thing, a personal crisis" (206). Now, it is of little consequence.

Having broken sacred southern taboos, Lumpkin—in the tradition of Huck Finn, after violating those same racial taboos—decides to go the whole hog. She returns to Dixie as the YWCA's national student secretary for the southern region, working with black colleagues, visiting black institutions, and attending black student conferences. She sees everything in a new light. Earlier she had paid little attention to segregated railroad cars; now she is struck by how demeaning Jim Crow cars are for African Americans: "Now I knew that I had rejected racial inferiority, and with it, the entire peculiar set of ways which it allegedly justified" (229). She could even think, "as perhaps I still did at the time of my Southern remaking," that she "had banished the dominion of the past"—although, at other times, she suspected that some of "the unchanging" still clung to her (235).

Lumpkin concludes her narrative of racial conversion by asking why she, and not other southerners, was transformed: "Why, in my case, did I not hold to things as they were?" She offers as a partial explanation "the mysterious chemistry of individuality." She also considers circumstances, in particular the sojourn in the Sand Hills. She does not, however, even here, consider the fact that her awakening began within months of her father's death. Indeed, at the end, she attributes her transformation in part *to* certain values her parents, her father as well as her mother, instilled in her, "ideals" that "were potentially explosive taken in their combination—'Do your duty always,' 'Aid the weak and helpless' " (238). Finally, she points to religion and the manner in which it was turned on itself

so that its high authority was fallen back on to justify the very acts which our Southern teaching had told us were unjustifiable. Under religion's felt demand I could first profane the sacred tabernacle of

our racial beliefs and go on profaning it in subsequent years, until I
no longer felt the need to lean on any kind of authority, save that of
the demands of a common humanity. (238–39)

This ended both the education and the conversion of Katharine Du Pre
Lumpkin, and it was an education, if not a conversion, in some manner
more thoroughgoing than that of Lillian Smith.[21] At the time they wrote,
both women had turned the light of realism on the world of their fathers,
both had rejected a vertical southern religion and embraced a horizontal
one that preached the responsibilities of human beings to each other, both
had been transformed from racial segregationists into racial integrationists.
But Lumpkin may also have been awakened more fully than Smith to the
evils of class, as well as race, in the South and in the nation. In *Killers of the
Dream* Smith indeed took notice of class, as in her description of southern
history—drawing on W. J. Cash's interpretation in *The Mind of the
South*—as an economic struggle between "Mr. Rich White" and "Mr.
Poor White," but her psychological portrait of the white southern male—
attached to his black mammy as a child, crawling back to her when he was
confused or in trouble, taking as his lover a black woman who was his black
mammy in another form—presupposes a privileged white child who not
only *had* a mammy but also a refined, repressed mother who would make
that mammy look all the more warm and comforting by contrast. Such was
not the case with most white southerners, a fact that Lillian Smith recognized in the abstract but one that Lumpkin, with her formative experience
in the Sand Hills, her involvement with labor issues—and with laborers—
and her own brief experience as a factory worker, seemed to feel more
acutely. Lumpkin, on the other hand, addressed questions of gender less effectively than Smith. As Elizabeth Fox-Genovese has written, one finds "silences" in *The Making of a Southerner*,[22] and many of these silences—as we

21. Lumpkin's education, as far as *The Making of a Southerner* is concerned, concludes
in the 1920s. In fact, her development as racial liberal and feminist continued long after
that, until her death in Chapel Hill in 1988. In 1974, when she was seventy-six, her biography of the abolitionist Angelina Grimké was published by the University of North Carolina
Press.

22. Elizabeth Fox-Genovese, "Between Individualism and Community: Autobiographies of Southern Women," in Berry, ed., *Located Lives,* 34. One encounters those same "silences" in reconstructing Lumpkin's life as well. According to Jacquelyn Dowd Hall, before

have also seen with Smith—concern her sexuality. The other primary silence of each concerned her father. Both Smith and Lumpkin could—and did—change their views of race, religion, and the "sacred" southern past; they could also see, in broad terms, the destructive effects of southern patriarchy; but they could never bring themselves, save in a sentence or two in *Killers of the Dream* and a single scene in *The Making of a Southerner*, to voice open criticism of their fathers, and more important, they never fully addressed the effect of their fathers on themselves. But the remarkable fact is that their books, in all other respects, were as bold and honest as they were. On the subject of race, both works are eloquent testimonies to the power of transformation—through religion, through education, through sheer will. Narratives of conversion, they also became, in their ways, *instruments* of conversion for other readers in that dark age of segregation that the southern 1940s continued to be.

Lumpkin's death she destroyed much of her private correspondence as well as her sister Grace's diary. And when Hall, in an interview with Lumpkin in 1974, turned the subject to her personal life, Lumpkin "resisted, politely but firmly, with a fixed and practiced resolve" (Hall, "Open Secrets," 119).

II

GOD'S DETERMINATION

James McBride Dabbs, Sarah Patton Boyle, Will Campbell

JAMES MCBRIDE DABBS of Rip Raps Plantation, South Carolina, was certainly not the first southerner to hold a providential view of southern history, nor to see the American South, despite all its shortcomings, as God's redemptive community. From early southern apologists such as the Calvinist Robert Lewis Dabney—who saw the South as a latter-day Israel and southerners as God's Chosen—and the mid-nineteenth-century social analyst Daniel Hundley to late-century Methodist divine Atticus Haygood—even to such notable twentieth-century fictional characters as Faulkner's Isaac McCaslin and Quentin Compson—God has been at the center of the southern picture. "A righteous God, for our sins toward Him," wrote Dabney, "has permitted us to be overthrown by our enemies and His." "We honestly believe . . . God had a design in permitting the old Slave-trade," insisted Hundley, "a design to bless and benefit the human race." Haygood, forerunner of the twentieth-century southern school of guilt and shame, saw "God's hand" not only in slavery but also in "its termination": emancipation was "set down in the order of divine Providence." Or, as W. J. Cash wrote of the mind of the nineteenth-century white southerner, "Slavery and, indeed, everything that was, was [God's] responsibility."[1]

Thus it was not unusual in itself that James McBride Dabbs spoke of

1. Robert Lewis Dabney, *A Defence of Virginia and Through Her of the South* (New York, 1867), 356; Daniel R. Hundley, *Social Relations in Our Southern States* (1860; reprint, Baton Rouge, 1979), 288; Haygood, *Our Brother in Black*, 51, 54; and W. J. Cash, *The Mind of the South*, 84.

God's providence in the working of southern affairs and a divine mission for the South—an obligation ultimately to provide a model of racial harmony for the rest of the world. It was not unusual, historically considered, but it did seem somewhat curious in the mid- and late twentieth century that a southerner of extensive education and travel, acquainted with the ways of the world and immensely practical in his approach to problem-solving, would speak of southern providence so frequently and with such conviction. But Dabbs, Presbyterian and humanitarian, did affirm more than once, as Atticus Haygood had before him, that Africans were brought to the American South to test and teach white southerners, to show them their own limitations and to prepare them through suffering to provide a spiritual example for a troubled world. However, Dabbs—like the seventeenth-century Puritans before him, struggling to fathom the relationship between God's determination and man's responsibility—was convinced that man, though his freedom of will, had to *choose* to repent of his past racial sins and live a new life of racial reconciliation. As sociologist Edgar T. Thompson wrote of Dabbs's work, "In the manner of the prophets of the Old Testament, he is calling upon the people of this region to face up to their racial as well as their individual sins, and to repent."[2]

But Dabbs was not only racial prophet; he was racial convert as well, and he tells the story of his transformation in three works of highly personal social and cultural commentary, *The Southern Heritage* (1958), *Who Speaks for the South?* (1964), and *Haunted By God* (1972), as well as in his remarkable spiritual autobiography, *The Road Home* (1960). Born in rural South Carolina in 1896, he was—like Lillian Smith and Katharine Du Pre Lumpkin—the grandchild of slaveowners and the child of parents who considered themselves exemplars of *noblesse oblige*. Not nearly so aware in his early life of racial injustice as Smith, in his published recollections Dabbs describes his childhood South as a *brighter* place than Smith remembered, a land of charm and pleasures. Indeed, this future racial iconoclast—who would become president of the racially progressive Southern Regional Council and a strong ally of the Civil Rights Movement—would continue to extol the charms and pleasures of southern life in a manner and with a

2. Edgar T. Thompson, Foreword to Dabbs's *Haunted By God* (Richmond, 1972), 7. *Haunted By God* (as HBG) hereafter cited by page number in the text.

frequency rare for certain of his fellow members of the party of southern racial guilt. In his celebration of rural life—particularly in an essay, "The Land," in that loyalist southern volume *The Lasting South* (1957)—as well as in his fear of industrialism and his rage against abstraction, Dabbs resembles in many ways the southern liberals' ideological adversaries, the Southern Agrarians. But not on the matter of race. In that particular Dabbs was as firm as Lillian Smith, a noncompromiser who came to believe that racial segregation was "evil" and that white southerners were not only oppressing a race but also endangering their own souls by condoning and participating in its oppression.

Dabbs's own racial conversion, as he describes it in the earliest of his books, *The Southern Heritage* and *The Road Home*, came much later than that of Smith and Lumpkin. As a child he had "a nostalgic sense of the Lost Cause," inherited from his mother, and, on race, accepted the position of his father: "there was no race question; it had been settled, nailed down for good by segregation, disfranchisement, and Plessy *vs.* Ferguson."[3] Looking back in his early sixties, he remembers his own early transgressions. Like both Lillian Smith and Katharine Lumpkin, he recalls encountering black children on a path and pushing them out of the way. (Indeed, such territorial competition, reported by a number of repentant southerners, becomes nearly a convention of the racial conversion narrative.) He recalls, in particular, meeting a black girl "much larger than I" who apparently was not going to move; "I drew back and hit her hard in the stomach." "I wasn't ashamed," Dabbs recalls, "but I didn't tell Father or Mother" (*SH*, 11).

Dabbs's conscience was not transformed as a college undergraduate (in his case, at the University of South Carolina) as Smith's and Lumpkin's had been, nor did his experience as a student outside the South change him. At Clark University in Massachusetts he was aware of "a Negro student or two on the campus," but "this was a strange land, and one might expect strange customs; I had gone there, after some effort and trouble, to study, and they weren't any of my business" (*SH*, 12). Dabbs felt the same way in France during World War I when "at a casual officers' mess . . . I looked up from

---

3. James McBride Dabbs, *The Southern Heritage* (New York, 1958), 7; and Dabbs, *The Road Home* (Philadelphia, 1960), 13. Both texts (as *SH* and *RH*) hereafter cited by page number in the text.

dinner to see a Negro lieutenant taking his seat opposite me." Although Dabbs felt strange, he decided, "I was over there to fight Germans, not to settle protocol on race matters (*SH,* 12). But he recalls, five years later, as a graduate student at Columbia University, mentioning to a classmate that he was grateful he did not have to sit next to a black woman in the class.

In fact, race was of little concern to Dabbs until his late thirties—and then for a reason that seemed at the time to have little to do with race. He was an English professor at Coker College in South Carolina, was married, and had two daughters. Life, as he describes it, had progressed pretty much as he had expected it to—until 1933, when his wife, after a long illness, died. "As a consequence of that disaster," Dabbs writes in *The Southern Heritage,* "there came to me a realization which had nothing to do with race directly but a lot to do with people" (*SH,* 13). He was awakened to his own suffering, and thus to other humans around him who suffered as well. In a search for answers after his wife's death, Dabbs experienced as well a "sense of spirit informing the entire world" (*RH,* 164). The church of his boyhood, though it had offered "good moral advice and maybe—being Presbyterian—sound theology," had not helped to "solve the mysteries of this life" (*HBG,* 250). His own struggles not only helped to solve such mysteries but also led him to ask questions that the southern church traditionally avoided: "Granted that the human-divine relationship is thus and so, what is the human relationship? How do men stand to one another?" (*RH,* 199).

Dabbs may have asked the question, but he did little to answer it for some time. Married again, he moved in the late 1930s back to the old Mc-Bride farm where he had grown up. His lone act of racial courage during the 1930s was writing a letter to a newspaper, voicing criticism of South Carolina governor Olin Johnston and the state legislature for their attempts to curb black voting—although his complaint, he later acknowledged, was not about their violation of human justice but rather about their "bad manners" (*SH,* 14). In a 1940 *Christian Century* article, "Is Christian Community Possible in the South?," Dabbs had concluded that such a community was not possible because of racial segregation. But, having called only for gradual change, he recognized later that he himself had continued to be a racial sinner: "I called myself a Christian and I practiced segregation" (*RH,* 223).

Compared with other white southerners, however, Dabbs was changing at breakneck speed. "I only sensed with vague uneasiness the fact that we [southerners] were haunted," he later wrote, "haunted by institutions and attitudes that, however vital in their inception, had now become pale and unreal" (*RH,* 218–19). Life "had pretty well stripped me of most of what I valued, and I saw that I didn't have much left but my basic humanity. . . . I was tired already." Segregation at first seemed to him "not so much an evil thing as a useless, foolish thing."[4] Being laid low, he was open to racial conversion. In essays on race in the *Christian Century* and other journals, and in pamphlets addressed to his fellow southerners, Dabbs explored his changing position. By the time he wrote *The Southern Heritage* in the 1950s, he had become fully aware of his racial sins and those of his homeland: "We were terribly wrong much of the time, and much of the time we knew it at the time, not merely in retrospect" (*SH,* 94); "We know we have done wrong, and we fear retaliation" (*SH,* 99). Sounding very much like Lillian Smith in *Killers of the Dream,* Dabbs announces, "I had finally to oppose all division and separation, both within myself and within that outer picture of myself, the world. When finally I realized what a division segregation was, I had to oppose it too" (*RH,* 228). In spite of his belief that segregation was "evil," Dabbs had already begun to take refuge in that conviction that increasingly was to inform his writing: "The more I think about the South and our problem here, the more sure I am that despite all appearances we have been blessed by the grace of God" (*RH,* 237).

Dabbs had hoped for a southern audience in *The Southern Heritage* and had identified with his presumed southern reader. Describing himself as "a Southerner slowed down by racial fog but determined to find a way out" (*SH,* 3), he had adopted a patient tone, considering every argument for segregation and then refuting it. Indeed, he had demonstrated his traditional southern loyalties in ways he had not intended: in celebrating southern leisure he had seemed to romanticize the "Negro stretched out [on a hot July afternoon] in the blazing sun on the bare floor of his cabin porch, asleep" (*SH,* 180); and in trying to explain the mind of the antebellum southern planter, he had reasoned, "It would never have occurred to him to justify cruelty, except as a disciplinary measure" (*SH,* 138). For a Calvinist, Dabbs

---

4. James McBride Dabbs, quoted in John Egerton, *A Mind to Stay Here: Profiles from the South* (New York, 1970), 37–38.

did not fully understand the capacity for evil in some of his fellow southerners past and present. As he later acknowledged, he had rather "polish . . .
the pinnacles of heaven" than "stok[e] the fires of hell" (*HBG*, 251).

In fact, *The Southern Heritage*, despite its wisdom, is not so insightful,
nor even in the end so personal, as Dabbs's next book, *Who Speaks for the
South?* Certainly his finest work, the book's misleading title is one of its few
weaknesses; it is clear that Dabbs himself speaks both for and to the South.
In the first two-thirds of the book he attempts a study similar in many respects to W. J. Cash's *The Mind of the South*, examining the mind and heart
of the antebellum white southerner, then the postbellum southerner, trac-
ing the influence of race, class, and religion in the Old South, the curious
mixture of innocence and guilt, the interaction of low country and Pied-
mont, of early English planters and ascendant "Southern Puritans," the
Scots-Irish. Dividing his book into three sections corresponding to
Cash's—"The Formation of Southern Character," "Its Bitter Testing"
(treating military defeat and Reconstruction), and "Its Present Possibility"—Dabbs wrote perhaps the most perceptive study of the southern
mind since Cash's 1941 *opus*. Lacking the stirring cadences and rhetorical
flourishes of his fellow Carolinian, he was nonetheless superior to Cash in
his discussion of certain matters: southern Calvinism, the presumed southern fury against abstraction, the relationship between shame and guilt in
the southern psyche, and, in most respects, the mind of the black southerner—in whom Cash was interested only insofar as the African American
helped to shape the white southern mind.

But it is not Dabbs's examination of the southern mind and psyche, no
matter how penetrating, in which I am principally interested. It is rather, in
the final chapters of his book, Dabbs himself as an example of that mind at
work—a southerner burdened with the sins of his fathers, bearing an inor-
dinate share of regional racial guilt, holding to a providential view of southern history, and appearing to be nothing less than a real-life Isaac McCaslin, although a more effective one. McCaslin, in Faulkner's "The Bear," sits
in the commissary of his family's plantation and attempts to come to terms
with the southern past and his family's role in it. God had "permitted"
white southerners to own both slaves and land, Isaac McCaslin had concluded, "land already accursed" but also blessed—"this land which He still
intended to save because He had done so much for it." The Civil War had

been God's determination as well: white southerners could "learn nothing save through suffering."[5] Isaac McCaslin, in Faulkner's story, was meditating in the 1880s on southern racial guilt; three-quarters of a century later we find James McBride Dabbs, living in the house of *his* slaveholding ancestors, also confessing the sins of the white South and professing the same providential theory of southern history.

Dabbs's confession, however, is not only for the sins of past generations but also for his own generation. It was not sufficient "to admit that our fathers failed, that slavery was a mistake, that the Confederacy was properly defeated."[6] It was necessary as well "to admit that we ourselves have failed; that we should not have permitted the racial injustice to go on; that we have been selfish, overprudent, cowardly. No matter how the blame should be distributed, we have failed." Despite the South's sins, and his own, Dabbs is convinced that his homeland can still be saved because of "God's grace"—and because, further, God has intended the South to be a "pilot project" in human brotherhood. Divine providence, Dabbs asserts with all the assurance of a seventeenth-century Puritan, had always been in the southern picture:

> [God] was in the picture, in the patience and trusting faith of the Negro, and in the acceptance of life as imperfect and sinful on the part of the white. He remained in the picture through the South's defeat, willing that defeat and the great lessons it spread before us. He was with the Negro when he was shoved aside through segregation, into a sort of Babylonian captivity, where, partly because he was out of the mainstream, he could both retain the best of the past and prepare through long, hard years for the future. (379)

Finally, Dabbs, just as the fictional McCaslin, places his faith in the black southerner as a kind of redeemer—and his is a conviction that we shall see echoed by other race-burdened white southerners in the years to come. In the words of Isaac McCaslin, black southerners are "better than we are. Stronger than we are"; they will "outlast us," will "endure." Or in

5. Faulkner, "The Bear," 256, 277, 280, 287.
6. James McBride Dabbs, *Who Speaks for the South?*, 377. Hereafter cited by page number in the text.

Dabbs's words, "The Negro is wiser," has "accepted better" the tragedy of life, "admits it, talks about it" (376–77), and, besides, has brought a heretofore absent "moral urgency" into the public life of the South (359). Dabbs sees in the Civil Rights Movement a phenomenon nearly biblical in its drama:

> A despised minority, excluded from the common life, returns at last more in love than in hatred to reveal to the majority, not only that possibility of community that has always haunted the mind of the South, but also and far more importantly a vision of the universal meaning of failure and defeat, revealing how men become human through the positive acceptance and affirmation of defeat. The man who was once servant reveals through his suffering to the man who was once master the meaning of suffering. (381).

The Negro as savior: such was, in essence, Dabbs's message. The black southerner could redeem the southern church, the southern body politic, the white southern soul. Black southerners themselves, in the era of the Civil Rights Movement, may have sensed more pressing needs: voting rights, public accommodations, equal access to housing and employment. When one was fighting for the right to use a water fountain or public restroom, redeeming the soul of the white southerner might have seemed a high-minded extravagance. And Dabbs, a practical man as well as a spiritual one, would have understood that reasoning. Still, as a moral historian and a believer in God's determination, he was compelled to take the long view.

He was to take that same view in his final book, *Haunted By God,* a work whose lack of polish and whose place in the Dabbs chronicle can both be attributed to the same fact: the author died the day—May 30, 1970—he completed the initial draft. By this time Dabbs, the Presbyterian layman, had become virtually the racial prophet, and his text was "Inasmuch as ye have done it unto one of the least of these . . . ye have done it unto me." Again, he saw the need for a general southern repentance: "Except for so-called personal religion, this cry ["Against thee, thee only, have I sinned!"] has until recently been absent from the South. We haven't admitted that we need to be reconciled to God in our society" (*HBG,* 178). Indeed, even more openly than before, Dabbs was bold to declare, "I am finally concerned to understand history as an expression, direct or indirect, of the will of God" (*HBG,* 133).[7]

Finally, as Lillian Smith's was, Dabbs's crusade for racial justice in the middle years of the century was about far more than race. He had undertaken that crusade in the first place after sensing the general pain and suffering in life following the death of his wife, and he had realized at that time how little the religious faith of his fathers sustained him. The church of his youth had, quite simply, not given him "God." What he found in his pursuit of racial justice did give him God, and if he idealized the sense of interracial community that would come out of the struggle for equal rights, he was hardly the only one who erred in that direction. His ultimate goal was the same kind of "wholeness" Lillian Smith had sought, and the breaking down of barriers that he and his fathers had erected was a large step in that direction.

7. The year Dabbs completed *Haunted By God,* another southern philosopher-agrarian—who, like Dabbs, had strayed from home and then returned to farm and write—produced a book that also pondered race and religion and likewise concluded that the "moral" aspects of Christianity had been overwhelmed by the "mystical"—and that the moral needed to reassert itself. However, Wendell Berry of Kentucky, poet, novelist, and essayist, speaks not of "evil," "awakening," and "conversion" but rather employs a medical metaphor to describe the South's condition: racism is "a hidden wound," a wound both historical and deeply personal, "as complex and deep in my flesh as blood and nerves" (*The Hidden Wound* [Boston, 1970], 2). Heretofore "unwilling . . . to open in myself" that wound (1), he writes now because he wants "to know, as fully and exactly as I can, what the wound is and how much I am suffering from it. And I want to be cured" (2). But, Berry maintains, he cannot be fully cured: "doomed by . . . history" of region and family—he too is descended from slaveholders on both sides—he will be "if not always a racist, then a man always limited by the inheritance of racism (63).

At the time he wrote, Berry had not pondered racism nearly so long and hard as Dabbs had—he was but thirty-six, nearly forty years younger than Dabbs—but in sections of *The Hidden Wound* he sounds remarkably like Dabbs. After recounting his own racial history—he does not itemize early racial sins as Dabbs does but rather focuses largely on his affection for an older black worker on the family farm—he acknowledges, as Dabbs had, that in his early years he was "passive" as regards race: he had not "knowingly mistreated or insulted any black person because he was black," but neither had he dealt with "the question" of race (115). He concludes, again as Dabbs customarily did in his volumes on race, by insisting that white Americans must acknowledge moral responsibility, must seize the initiative, must "free" both blacks and whites, and regain "our own humanity" (144).

In 1962, four years after the publication of Dabbs's *The Southern Heritage* and two years before *Who Speaks for the South?* appeared a book, *The Desegregated Heart*, by Virginian Sarah Patton Boyle, who brought to her writing no particular credentials other than what had been over the previous decade a wholehearted commitment to equal rights for African Americans. Her book was a curious specimen indeed, part racial conversion narrative and part retreat from the battle into which that conversion had thrust her. In its first three-quarters, Boyle's narrative was more intense than anything James McBride Dabbs ever wrote, but Boyle, worn down by her total commitment to human rights in a region that fought her every step of the way, finally lacked the staying power of Dabbs, Lillian Smith, and Katharine Du Pre Lumpkin. She did not backslide so much as find refuge, several years later, in a more conventional brand of salvation, and at that point, as far as race was concerned, she fell silent. *The Desegregated Heart* received a modest amount of attention when it appeared in the early 1960s; a decade later, at least outside the Old Dominion, Boyle was forgotten, and in obscurity she would remain.[8]

If Sarah Patton Boyle was, in her writing, one of the most fervent of southern racial converts of the 1950s and 1960s, it was in part because she had so far to come, so much to repent. The daughter of an Episcopal church official and granddaughter of Confederate veterans who had been close to Lee, Stonewall Jackson, and J. E. B. Stuart—as well as the direct descendant of still another Virginian who had been a general in the American Revolution—Sarah Patton was born in 1906 on the ancestral plantation near Charlottesville. Educated at home and, in her teens, at the Corcoran School of Art in Washington, leading an early life that was altogether conventional and unremarkable, she married at twenty-six a well-bred Marylander who became a professor at the University of Virginia. She had two sons, began to write on occasion for magazines, and settled into a comfortable life as faculty wife and community benefactor. In truth, there seemed little, other than her superior breeding, to distinguish Patty Boyle

8. Biographical information on Boyle (other than that from *The Desegregated Heart*) taken from John Egerton, *A Mind to Stay Here,* 128–45, the finest introduction to Boyle's life and work, and the research of Charles F. Irons of the University of Virginia.

from others in the Charlottesville community—until, in 1950, in her mid-forties, she suddenly and dramatically took her stand against racial segregation and brought down upon herself the wrath of Virginia's old guard. It is the story of her struggles, as well as of the change of mind that brought her to a racial transformation, that Boyle tells in *The Desegregated Heart*. She undertook her struggle and, later, wrote her book because, she believed, "as a white Southerner I was partially responsible for the inequities which Negroes suffer . . . it was my responsibility, and therefore my right, to atone."[9]

The Desegregated Heart follows, in its first quarter, the approximate pattern of Katharine Lumpkin's *The Making of a Southerner*—except that, unlike Lumpkin, Boyle announces her transformation in the beginning: "My primary purpose in this book is to share my discovery that to have joy and peace we must love. . . . My secondary purpose is to explain what induced me, although I was raised as a typical white Southerner, to take my stand with Negroes against the white South" (xi). But after that statement of intent Boyle turns, as Lumpkin did in her early chapters, to a description of a nearly idyllic South. Immediately she lets the reader know that her grandfather had owned four thousand acres and 163 slaves and that (as if there were any doubt) her family belonged to the "Southern aristocracy"; in fact, her mother and grandmother told her "that our family was the best in Virginia" (3–4). As with Lumpkin's, her family's Episcopalianism, though staunch, meant less than their true religion, the southern way of life: "The South and what we thought of her, her ideals and her people, were more precious to us than anything we learned in church" (8).

Like Lumpkin as well, at the same time she speaks highly of her family, Boyle undermines her favorable description of her parents, indeed her entire portrait of a southern paradise. Lumpkin's father had been her racial mentor; Boyle's mother is hers. Boyle notes the Pattons' affection for their black servants, their sense of *noblesse oblige*—but then reports that her mother complained of paying the cook and other help the paltry wage she did. "My mother must have been a rather hard taskmistress," Boyle adds, "for we never kept a cook long" (15). Similarly, a black farmhand, young Patty's "dearest friend," was dismissed because, according to Mrs. Patton,

---

9. Sarah Patton Boyle, *The Desegregated Heart* (New York, 1962), 118. Hereafter cited by page number in the text.

he had become too "shiftless and uppity . . . and on top of that he had the nerve to ask for a raise" (19).

Although paying homage in these early pages to the charms and pleasures of plantation life, Boyle is not as successful as Lumpkin in concealing her later feelings. She speaks of her family's "loathsome sense of social superiority" (5), a family trait for which Boyle may later repent but which she herself never truly overcomes. After introducing her parents, Boyle turns—in a manner that is nearly formulaic in racial confession narratives—to a litany of her own racial sins, which are also, of course, the sins of her family. It "was assumed by every member of my family that a Negro's word was unreliable," she reports (17), and it was "taken for granted" that Negroes smelled bad (13); indeed, "my thoughts became saturated with the assumption that Negroes belonged to a lower order of man than we" (14). She reflects, in particular, on her family's live-in black servant, who was given a room with "a slave-quarters atmosphere" (12): "That a Negro might yearn for an attractive room even though—or perhaps especially because—she had none in her own home simply never entered our minds. It was assumed that they lived on a lower level than whites, desiring nothing better" (13).

Her recognition of these early assumptions is painful enough for the fifty-year-old Boyle, looking back, but the memory that is most painful is that of her parents' mandate, on her twelfth birthday, that her relations with blacks must henceforth be "formal." "A dreadful training period" ensued, Boyle reports, during which "I was watched and rebuked if I forgot any of the many taboos which suddenly came into being" (21). The training "called for repression not only of what was happiest in the years just passed, but also of much that was natural and dear in my human contacts as well" (21–22). "All that had been best in my life was branded WRONG," she writes. "It was RIGHT to do what I dimly sensed was contrary to the laws of love and loyalty—to set a wall between myself and friends, to meet overtures with formality—these things were RIGHT" (22). Again, then, a southern child, in the tradition of Huck Finn, experiences a battle between sound heart and deformed conscience, and as with Lillian Smith and Lumpkin before her, the deformed conscience wins—at the time. When a black friend of whom she was very fond asks Patty—now "Miss Patty" to her friend—to play, and Patty answers stiffly "No, I can't," her mother observes and commends her: "That was a good girl." "A strange combination of depression and pride swept me," Boyle recalls. "I was a GOOD GIRL. But oh, what had I *done!*" (22).

Once her training period is over, Boyle is a product of the "code": "I loved Negroes and, in my segregated way, respected and admired them as individual human personalities," but "when a Negro didn't 'keep his place' I felt outraged. . . . My indignation was triggered by a sense of guilt. I had learned that equality relations with Negroes were WRONG, and that it was my fault if a Negro attempted them." But despite her belief that African Americans lacked the "Anglo-Saxon virtues" of industry, chastity, and honor, Boyle continued to feel "more at home with them, than with my closest white friend" (30). As an "individual," she "loved Negroes and believed they loved me. I believed that between Negroes and my whole stratum of Southern society there was a continuous flow of understanding, love, tenderness, and well-wishing" (36).

The conditioning of Boyle's childhood held sway for another twenty years. Even when she leaves home and moves to Washington for art school, she cannot escape the old patterns. She employs as a maid a young black woman with whom she becomes so familiar that the maid calls Boyle by her first name:

> I felt my entire interior congeal. A Negro had failed to call me Miss! *And I was as guilty as she.* How unseemly my attitude must have been to invite such a thing! I experienced a terrible wave of depression, mixed with a kind of horror of myself, as though I had suddenly stumbled on the discovery that I possessed some repellent abnormality. . . . I must have somewhere let our relationship become an equality one. (40)

In the nights following, Boyle's sleep "was tormented by a frighteningly dark and ugly cloud of guilt": "My mother had warned me about this. . . . 'This sort of thing' must be stopped at once. It would be WRONG not to stop it—WRONG for her, as well as for me and the South." *Why* it was wrong "wasn't clear" to Boyle, "and it didn't occur to me to analyze it," but she felt "as a small child feels when caught in some enormous breach of the family's moral code" (40). Finally she decides she has "only one way out": when she next sees the maid, she instructs the woman not to call her again by her first name. To "make the rebuke a little less personal," Boyle had added the words "People might not understand" (40–41). But she had seen the rejection in the eyes of the woman who had been her friend.

Such an incident "should have made me question the perfection of our Southern way of life" (43), Boyle reasons, but it did not. Neither did another incident that in many ways parallels the young Lillian Smith's childhood encounter with the girl, assumed to be white and discovered to be "colored," who briefly lived in the Smith home. Boyle befriends a fellow student at the Corcoran, indeed could not "recall ever being so quickly and fully drawn to another personality." But the friendship comes to an abrupt end when the young woman, "with a deeply wounded look in her eyes," comes by to tell Boyle she is leaving school. At first Boyle wonders why she is leaving, then a few weeks later, while attending an address given by Boyle's father at Howard University, she sees the young woman and realizes: "Though she looked white, she was a Negro, and had been found out." Again, Boyle isn't sure how to respond: "How wrong of her to practice such a deception! Yet how awful that she had to leave school for such a reason!" (41). After the service Boyle wants to walk up to the young woman and speak, "but not knowing what to say I didn't approach her" (42).

After Boyle married and moved to Charlottesville, she continued to hold to the old prejudices. Or, rather, "It was as though water purifier had been put into a contaminated reservoir but left in sealed bottles." Interracial encounters such as those she had experienced in Washington "were little centers—bottles—of genuine truth and experience which remained sealed off by my indoctrination and training, unable to permeate and purify my overall conception of the Negro people and their situation in the South" (43). Such continued to be the case for Boyle throughout the 1930s and 1940s—until in 1950, in her forties, she experienced what she called a sudden "awakening" (48). The catalyst for that awakening was the breaking of the color line at the University of Virginia. When Boyle's husband told her that a young African American had applied to the law school and, through the courts, would almost certainly be admitted, she felt "lighter": "Although I hadn't known it, my chest had been in a plaster cast and now was sawed free. I could breathe!" (50). She felt that "something lovely, lost in childhood, quietly awaited recovery. Long-buried yearnings might now be satisfied. . . . I felt as displaced persons must feel when news comes that soon they will see longlost kin. . . . Everything of greatest worth in my life seemed centered here" (52). To employ the metaphor to which Boyle often returns, "The tidal wave swept into my private reservoir, banging my sealed bottles together until they broke, releasing my captive insight into the general stream of my thought" (50).

At the same time Boyle felt "relief" from racial guilt, she also experienced "sudden guilt pangs" of another sort: "I was filled with shame for violating the code" (50). The two impulses—to welcome the student's admission but also to fear it—battled within her, as they had often before. In her mind Boyle views her own past racial transgressions; she also sees, "as though it were a color print, the face of Tobe, the hired hand at whose firing I fell ill. It was as though a dam burst with the waters of longing for all that I had lost along with him" (51). This time she would take action as she had not before. She writes a letter to the applicant, twenty-six-year-old Gregory Swanson from Danville, addresses him as "Mr. Swanson" (a bold step for her as it had been for Lumpkin), and welcomes him to the University of Virginia.

"It was awful thoughts and awful words, but they was said": thus spoke Huck Finn after he had just chosen "forever, betwixt two things," had violated white racial codes, and had decided not to turn Jim in.[10] Patty Boyle was a little more restrained and, given her station, a little more grammatical, but her reaction had the same moral significance: "I felt good. I had said what I wanted to say." Finally washed free of racial sin (and, unlike Huck, knowing she was), Boyle thus began her career as apostate. Hers was at first, however, a most uncertain apostasy. When she received the student's response, saying—in Boyle's words—"he was looking forward to our being great friends and to many other enjoyable relationships at the University," something "gripped [Boyle] with digging, cold fingers." "This implied social equality!" she realized; "clearly I had already made Swanson FORGET HIS PLACE!" (58). So she had written a second letter distancing herself to some extent—and, after he had won his suit for admission, a third, this time offering to help him find a place to live "in the Negro community" (61), cautioning him not to "move too fast" (62), and telling him he should be grateful for what had already been accomplished. Boyle is surprised when, upon receiving that letter, Swanson becomes cool to her.

10. Mark Twain, *Adventures of Huckleberry Finn*, 200.

In fact, Boyle was nowhere near so tough-minded as Lillian Smith and Katharine Lumpkin, not nearly so knowledgeable, not nearly so aware of either white racial intransigence or black suspicions of well-meaning whites. Her initial racial conversion was, in some measure, the easier part of her journey; much more difficult was deciding what form her new commitment should take. Her involvement with Gregory Swanson in the following months, as well as her larger efforts on behalf of desegregation in Virginia, seem at times a comedy of errors. When she shows Swanson an article she has written on his admission to the university and sees "hostility, fury" on his face, she realizes that her piece "dripped sentimental maternalism" (72–73). When she entitles another article "We Want a Negro at the UVA," she is surprised at the adverse black reaction—until she realizes that black Virginians want more than *one* African American at the university. And when Boyle approaches a black newspaper editor in Charlottesville to seek his advice, she is disappointed that he, though supportive, is cool to her.

In telling her story, Boyle is not hesitant to admit to the reader just how blind she has been. Recognizing even earlier, in some measure, her innocence, she had asked the black editor, T. A. Sellers, to counsel her on race relations, and he had agreed. For many months she visits his office "for instruction," and though his face "habitually wore an angry bitter look," he "taught" her about race from an African American's point of view—taught her so well, in fact, that she dedicated *The Desegregated Heart* to Sellers. "His paternalism was like balm," writes Boyle. "I fell easily into the relationship of a white child under the authority and supervision of a Negro adult" (103). Her use of the word "paternalism" is telling: roles are being reversed, or, rather, in one particular, for this child of plantation privilege, the roles are familiar after all. Boyle doesn't mention Uncle Remus, but she might as well have—except this is a *new* Uncle Remus, one with an "angry bitter look," dispensing a new kind of advice to the privileged, plantation-bred white child.

It is *as* a child on several occasions that Boyle describes herself, and as a child that we are sometimes forced to see her—or, if not a child, at least as an emotionally insecure adult dependent altogether on the love and good will of African Americans. "I loved Negroes," she writes. "They were my people, more mine and in a truer sense than my own blood kin. I loved them and they loved me. We were part of each other" (51). African Ameri-

cans such as Swanson and Sellers might have taken issue with that assessment, might have heard the none-too-distant echoes of *white* paternalists,
from slaveowning days to the present, that they too "loved their Negroes."
But to Boyle a mutual expression of black-white affection was indispensable
to an emotionally satisfying life. It had been as well to Katharine Lumpkin,
who was distressed when the black laborers on her family's Sand Hills farm
were not warm to her. One could easily trace such feelings, in both cases, to
a privileged southern childhood, and I mean in ways that go beyond the desire for affection from a black mammy. Beyond that, expressions of affection and gratitude from black subordinates seemed to confirm that these
subordinates were not treated badly after all, were in fact happy in their ser-
vitude. Despite the success of Swanson's efforts to integrate the University
of Virginia, Boyle finds that she is disappointed, and she knows why: "My
image of Negroes as full of quick praise and appreciation for kindnesses was
dear to me, and my dependence on their approval was great" (176). To her,
Negroes were a "symbol of comfort, love, and security" (89); she had
"known no experience more distressing than the discovery that Negroes
didn't love me" (88).

To her credit, Boyle continued to fight for equal rights even after her
painful realization, and hers was a struggle that required a great deal of
courage in the Virginia of the early 1950s. But after "light broke in my
darkness" (115), as Boyle described her racial conversion, there was no
turning back—at least not for a very long time. She expanded her efforts
from Charlottesville and the university to the state as a whole, attending
NAACP meetings, speaking to other racially progressive groups, and writing articles as well as letters to editors and state leaders. After the Supreme
Court decision on school desegregation in 1954—which made her feel
"wonderfully free" (179)—she grew even bolder. When she published, in
1955, an article in the *Saturday Evening Post* titled "Southerners Will *Like*
Integration" (a title not of her making), she felt the full force of white
southern wrath—social ostracism, attacks in Virginia's editorial pages, calls
for her husband's dismissal from the university, harassing phone calls, and,
the following year, a six-foot cross burned on her lawn. At this point she experienced at least a partial awakening of another sort, one that suggests just
how much a product not only of race prejudice but also of southern class
prejudice she was. Up until 1954 she had believed that whites of her class

would support desegregation of the public schools, particularly if the federal government mandated it. She had echoed the self-serving claim on the part of privileged white southerners that the lower, uneducated classes were responsible for all southern racial troubles. The reaction to her *Saturday Evening Post* article should have taught her otherwise—particularly since some of the harshest editorial responses came from Virginians of high birth—but this was one lesson she never did learn fully. Writing in 1960, she still maintained that "the greater part of our race prejudice is vested in the lower classes" (208). Nor, writing in 1960, could she again refrain from reminding her readers that she came from "the First Families of Virginia." Patty Boyle, who came up from racism, could never come up from classism.

The last quarter of *The Desegregated Heart* departs from the optimistic and at times buoyant tone of the earlier chapters. Although Boyle continued to work in 1956 and 1957 for the Virginia Council on Human Relations, she grew increasingly discouraged with what she found: "My hope that 'the people' would rise up and recover the Southern Dream died a slow and groaning death" (279). In 1959, after the federal courts had struck down Virginia's plan of massive resistance to school desegregation, the state's public schools began to integrate. But Boyle found little joy: "All that I had fought for was lost. . . . I had not battled for the fact of integration. This was in the hands of judges and Constitutional lawyers, and was assured. I had expended my heart and strength, mind and soul for an integration accomplished with love and grace, courtesy and thanksgiving" (288). And this goal had not been accomplished. After 1959, she writes, her heart was a "void": She had "struck rock bottom," was "spiritually bankrupt" (293).

The final section of Boyle's book concerns her efforts to refill that void. It also suggests strongly that she had been altogether serious when she wrote in her prefatory note that her "secondary purpose" in *The Desegregated Heart* was to write about race—her "primary purpose" being to "share my discovery that to have joy and peace we must love" (xi). Indeed, race is barely mentioned in the book's final seventy-five pages, so intent is Boyle in describing her personal search for faith through other means. Having been reborn once, with her racial conversion in 1950 and her total immersion in civil rights, now in the late 1950s she is reborn again, and this time in a more conventional manner, through—in her words—"a personal relationship with Christ."[11] She writes that, in 1950, "when I felt called to serve, I broke loose from my self-center and had a feeling of being magically free" (320). But even after that racial transformation, even while she had been publicly virtuous, "I, too, had been guilty of all the heartless, vainglorious, deceitful, and cowardly acts I had seen done" (342–43). And now she must move on to redemption of another sort.

It would be overly cynical to maintain that racial involvement was, for Boyle, primarily a means to escape the prison of self, to find meaning and faith in an otherwise sterile world—or to contend that, in some measure, her story was the story, writ large, of many other southern racial converts. Who can, after all, fully judge motivation? And who can generalize? In Boyle's case, even after her disillusionment (far earlier than most others') with the Civil Rights Movement, she continued to take some part in it. In the early 1960s she participated in racial demonstrations in Richmond and Charlottesville, and in 1964—at the request of Martin Luther King, Jr., whom she greatly admired and who himself had praised *The Desegregated Heart*—she traveled to St. Augustine, Florida, to protest segregation in restaurants and other public accommodations, and she spent three days in jail for her efforts. In 1964 she also produced a short primer in race relations, *For Human Beings Only,* in which she dealt with practical concerns of integrated living. Finally, in 1966, she traveled to Mississippi to join the march that was begun in response to the shooting of James Meredith. But the "original idealism" of the Civil Rights Movement, Boyle felt, had begun to dissipate long before 1966, and with the Meredith march, its cries of black power, and what Boyle termed "a general sort of moral disintegration," she "saw nothing to live or die for in it."[12]

After that, her retreat from the civil rights arena was absolute. Her commitment from 1966 forward was, in some measure, a commitment to the old vertical southern religion, which eschewed a heavy involvement in social action, and Boyle experienced a loss of her earlier faith in the "inherent goodness in all men." She believed that "this nation could have been redeemed by the Negro people," but, because of their despair, it was not.[13]

11. Egerton, *A Mind to Stay Here,* 142.
12. Boyle, quoted in Egerton, *A Mind to Stay Here,* 139–42.
13. Boyle, quoted in Egerton, *A Mind to Stay Here,* 143.

Of *course* it was not, one might say; redemption is too great a task to assign to any one people of any color and station, and the Civil Rights Movement, despite its many achievements, could not accomplish that. But that possibility is what Boyle—as how many other racial converts to varying degrees?—envisioned at the time of her transformation in 1950. From the vantage point of the early 1960s she saw that earlier awakening as but a step, albeit a major one, in a greater quest for religious faith that brought her to the spiritual fulfillment she claims ultimately to have achieved. It is clear that her earlier experience and the resulting involvement with civil rights had freed her at least as much as it had freed black Virginians. At the end of *The Desegregated Heart,* Boyle describes herself as "free to be grateful and glad that I lost my life, and therefore found it; above all, free to love a little, thus gaining strength to seek, learn, and love a little more" (364).

Will Campbell was fully as high-minded as Sarah Patton Boyle and James McBride Dabbs when he chose to be; it's just that much of the time he preferred the role of folksy maverick, occasionally even court jester, to that of high moralist. A populist Baptist preacher who served for a while as chaplain at the University of Mississippi, then worked for the National Council of Churches and for a group called the Committee of Southern Churchmen, Campbell seemed to be everywhere during the Civil Rights Movement, living in Nashville, traveling to Little Rock, Birmingham, or wherever a racial crisis arose. Insisting later that he was never actually "part of the civil-rights movement," he nonetheless served—as John Egerton has written—as "mediator, strategist and adviser" for various civil rights groups as well as for nonaffiliated southerners of both races. Dressed in cowboy boots and western wear, likely as not chewing tobacco, given to picking up a guitar and playing when he felt like it, Campbell was a *character* of a distinctly southern variety, but he was much more than that. He was unlike any other prominent white integrationist of his day in that he kept avenues of discussion open to all southerners, Klansmen as well as civil rights workers. As distrustful of abstraction, theory, and "social engineering" as any Southern Agrarian, he thoroughly believed—in Egerton's words—in the "inherently evil nature of man." But he also believed, as much as James McBride Dabbs, in the grace of God. "You are forgiven"

was *his* theology—or, as his famous proclamation has it, "We are all bastards, but God loves us anyway."[14]

Campbell was a self-described "poor white"—one of "those called rednecks," he said elsewhere—descended from that breed in which, according to Patty Boyle, "the greater part of our racial prejudice is vested,"[15] although Campbell's case might call that generalization into question. Born on a small Mississippi farm in 1924, he spent much of his boyhood helping his older brother Joe with the plowing, planting, cultivating, and harvesting. Their father, on welfare for a while, was incapacitated with a heart murmur. Baptized at age seven, by his midteens Campbell had been ordained in the East Fork Baptist Church; at sixteen he preached his first sermon, holding a large pulpit Bible given to his church by the Ku Klux Klan and embossed with its insignia. After a year at Louisiana College, a Southern Baptist institution, Campbell joined the army and served as a medic in the South Pacific during World War II. He returned to take a degree at another Baptist college, Wake Forest in North Carolina, and after a further year of study at Tulane, he left for Yale Divinity School, where he gained both a B.D. degree and a number of lessons in regional and class consciousness. Returning to the South—first Louisiana, then Mississippi and Tennessee—he became (as he later described himself) "a missioner to the Confederacy, bridge between white and black, challenging the recalcitrant, exposing the gothic politics of the degenerate southland; prophet with a Bible in one hand and a well-worn copy of W. J. Cash in the other."[16] He paid a price for his apostasy, as nearly all racial apostates did. He was hurt by a favorite uncle's "bitter disappointment and displeasure that his own nephew had turned out to be a nigger lover and renegade preacher" (151). And in the early 1960s his father advised him not to come home to southern Mississippi for a visit, not because his father didn't want to see Campbell but because "he had learned from a neighbor that a local racist group had said if I came home that summer I would leave in a box" (241).

14. Egerton, *A Mind to Stay Here*, 15–31, esp. 21, 23, 31. Egerton's essay is the best introduction to Campbell's life and work.

15. Will Campbell, *Brother to a Dragonfly* (1977; reprint, New York, 1994), 97; Campbell, *Providence* (Atlanta, 1992), 23; and Boyle, *The Desegregated Heart*, 208. *Brother to a Dragonfly* hereafter cited by page number in text.

16. Will Campbell, *Forty Acres and a Goat* (Atlanta, 1986), 5.

Will Campbell's deep commitment to the cause of civil rights, then, is clear. But the question with Campbell is the same Katharine Lumpkin asked herself in *The Making of a Southerner:* why him? Sociologically speaking, one could hardly imagine a less promising beginning for one who would become a staunch advocate of racial justice—dirt poor, fundamentalist, born and raised in the state at the bottom of nearly all the nation's social and cultural indexes, and into a family near the bottom of even that state's white social scale, a family with no tradition of higher education, social outreach, general enlightenment, or *noblesse oblige.* But that, as Campbell saw it, was precisely the answer: he understood the oppressed, both black and white, because he had been oppressed himself. Part of the answer came as well from his three years away from home in World War II, looking from afar at the American South. And much of the answer came from a Christianity that developed from the salvation-centered religion of his youth into a faith that held that the greatest good one could perform was to help those in need. "The Christian view on race," Campbell wrote in 1962, "is the universal principle of the fatherhood of God and the brotherhood of man," and the "acute problem of race," he added (sounding very much like Lillian Smith), was "a symptom of man's estrangement from God and a symbol of the brokenness of the body of Christ." Thus, "the redemptive purpose of Jesus Christ and the judgment of God upon his people are more than distantly related to race relations. They are at the very heart and core of the solution."[17] The Civil Rights Movement, Campbell wrote, was "all part and parcel of my Christian commitment" (201).

These were the reasons Will Campbell threw himself into a crusade for human rights, and to Lillian Smith, Katharine Lumpkin, James McBride Dabbs, and Patty Boyle they would have appeared sound enough. Those were, in fact, the very reasons they themselves gave at various times for their own involvement. But Campbell's brother Joe, less high-minded, added another reason: "What you're saying is that you're going to use the niggers to save yourself." "Your niggers are like my pills," added the pharmacist Joe. "They prop you liberals up and make you feel good." Will Campbell did not want to think that, but he knew his brother "had hit a nerve" (201). Sometimes he questioned his own motives.

17. Will Campbell, *Race and the Renewal of the Church* (Philadelphia, 1962), 46–47.

Campbell's exchange with his brother comes in his most personal work, *Brother to a Dragonfly* (1977), a lament for his brother's tortured life that is at least as much his own memoir and racial conversion narrative as it is his brother's story. Joe Campbell had been his younger brother's hero—it was he who first left the farm and who introduced Will to a larger world—but Joe, ever generous and buoyant, led a hard life that culminated in an addiction to prescription drugs, periods of erratic behavior, and an early death. It is his story Will Campbell tells in *Brother to a Dragonfly*, but he tells as well the story of his own journey up from ignorance and prejudice. In fact, he often uses Joe as a sort of sounding board for his own ideas and as an audience for his own adventures and accomplishments, therefore letting the reader know even more about Will than about Joe Campbell.

In the beginning, *Brother to a Dragonfly* is not a book principally about race but rather about family, farm life, and religion. It was impossible, of course, for any Mississippian growing up in the 1920s and 1930s to be altogether unaware of race: Will remembers a black boy who helped out on the farm for five dollars a month, slept on a cot in the smokehouse, and played with the two Campbell boys—who became his friend but did not let him forget that he was still a kind of "slave rented, not bought" (29). Campbell also remembers from his childhood a black man who was shot by other black men; that the murderers went free taught Will that "crimes of black against black were not as serious as white against white" (64). But, for the most part, Campbell recalls:

> Race was not an issue when we were growing up. The prevailing system of racial relationships was never discussed. It was, I suppose, considered a permanent arrangement. There were, in reality, two parallel worlds, social, cultural and political, existing in one geographical location. There were schools for white children and schools for black children. It never occurred to anyone, except an occasional black person who kept it to himself, that it would ever be any other way.
>
> And there were churches. Churches were for white people. And then there was niggerchurch. Niggerchurch was a social institution and in our minds had nothing to do with Christianity or any other religion. (108)

The southern racial status quo went unchallenged in Campbell's own mind until he found himself during World War II in the South Pacific, while Joe was recuperating from a broken leg back in Mississippi. In one of his many letters to Will, Joe wrote "in long and anguished details of the suffering of black people since slavery." Will was surprised to read his brother's words; he considered himself no bigot, just one who "found no occasion to violate the behavioral norms of my Mississippi upbringing." Nonetheless, he decided to read a book Joe recommended, a work that his brother said would "turn [his] head around" (96). *Freedom Road,* by Howard Fast, was hardly great literature, but Campbell was moved as he had never been before by the Reconstruction story of an illiterate former slave—whose "economic situation sounded at times like our own family history of that period" (96–97)—who lost his life trying to ensure racial justice. As Campbell finished the book on a hot Sunday morning in the Pacific, he realized:

> They were the most powerful and compelling words I had read in my nineteen years. The poor whites . . . were my people. And I knew that the black men and women . . . were those we grew up thinking we had to oppose. I had never questioned why we were so taught before, that it was because for us to do otherwise would constitute a threat to those who ruled us before the Civil War and who had in just one decade after the war succeeded in ruling us again. (97)

When he finished that book, Campbell writes thirty years later, he "knew that [his] life would never be the same": "I knew that the tragedy of the South would occupy the remainder of my days. It was a conversion experience comparable to none I had ever had, and I knew it would have to find expression" (98).

It is improbable that one book was responsible for this "conversion experience" on Campbell's part; more likely, the book simply brought to the surface thoughts and feelings that had lain dormant for some time and would have found expression soon enough. In any event, when he returned from the South Pacific, Campbell was a changed man. He began his odyssey out of the Deep South for education, only to return to Mississippi almost a decade later, this time with a mission to convert others not only to salvation-centered Christianity but also to human brotherhood. His timing could not have been more auspicious. Arriving at the University of Mississippi in 1954, three months after the Supreme Court decision on school desegregation, he ran into a caldron of white racial defiance. And Campbell quickly discovered that the leaders in defiance, the founders of the White Citizens Council, were not those who—in Campbell's words—"could be called ignorant rednecks or any of the other names which have so often been used to identify southern racists." They were, rather, a Harvard-educated lawyer, a prominent banker, and other leaders "not only . . . in business and commerce" but also "in culture and learning" (111).

Campbell managed to get himself in a great deal of trouble over the next two years—first for having in his home the black journalist Carl Rowan, who was passing through town; then for socializing (playing ping-pong qualified as such) with a local black minister; and for a number of other actions that violated racial etiquette. The greatest trouble, however, came in 1956, the year Campbell "took on the University administration, the State Legislature, and the mores of the South to help other people"—and, he adds, "to make me feel good" (112–13). His primary transgression was attempting to mix Christianity and race at an event called Religious Emphasis Week, a major occurrence on the Ole Miss campus. It is not that Campbell tried to invite African Americans to speak—but he did invite a liberal Episcopal priest who had given money to the NAACP, and that was enough to cause the university chancellor to send out a campus policeman to escort Campbell to the chancellor's house, where he encountered "a circle of about a dozen men, quiet and solemn faces" (119). When Campbell refused to disinvite the priest—and proceeded to coordinate a campaign in which all other invited speakers canceled in protest, then worked behind the scenes to sabotage the diluted version of Religious Emphasis Week—both Campbell and the University of Mississippi felt it was time for him to leave. When he received an offer to be a race relations worker in the South for the National Council of Churches, he accepted it.

The remainder of *Brother to a Dragonfly* consists of two strands of narrative running side by side, Campbell's accounts of his battle against southern racism and of his struggles to help Joe with drug addiction and marital problems. The structure of the book appears at times somewhat contrived: the author has Joe ask him to "tell me about some of the folks you visited in prison" (163), and Will obliges with stories of Martin Luther King, Ralph Abernathy, John Lewis, and other civil rights leaders, taking "a verbal journey around the South to where various people had been locked up for their involvement in civil rights demonstrations" (164). He also tells Joe, and thus the reader, about being summoned to Washington by Robert Kennedy, whose understanding of race and the South, Campbell suggests, was vastly inferior to his own. In all of this there is something a little self-indulgent: Campbell *knows* he is a character, a southern phenomenon. But there is much that is moving as well; at the end, the story comes back to Joe, to the East Fork Baptist Church cemetery, back to the beginning.

In the following two decades Will Campbell was to write several other books, at least a couple of a quasi-confessional nature. His memoir *Forty Acres and a Goat* (1986), despite its amusing title and a number of humorous episodes, contains an underlying streak of sadness, stemming largely from Campbell's sense, shared by a number of other white participants in the Civil Rights Movement, that the spirit of "beloved community" informing that movement had gone forever. "There is estrangement in the air," he writes in the mid-1980s. "And anger. There is more social segregation today than there was fifteen years ago." Or, as he says to a black friend, "You were an old fashioned integrationist. So was I. . . . But we are losing. . . . Or have we lost already?" If so, Campbell can at least recall his earlier feelings when he thought the movement had succeeded, when he experienced a sense of liberation he had never felt before. As he says to a black minister and friend, another veteran of the movement, "You gave me my freedom. I'm sorry I couldn't do more to give you yours." "I know I am more free than when it began," Campbell adds. "The Civil Rights Movement may be over for black people. It is far from over for whites."[18]

Like Sarah Patton Boyle before him, Campbell was reading the movement, of course, in white terms, was missing keenly the sense of interracial cooperation, even brotherly love, he had felt in the early 1960s, and he was assuming for that reason that the movement had somehow failed—when, in fact, it had succeeded in so many ways that were of immense practical (that is, social and political) value to black southerners. But Campbell's business, after all, was saving souls—for this world at least as much as for the next—and although his own soul might have been saved, in part, through his racial transformation, he had come to believe such was not the case for most of his fellow white southerners.

18. Campbell, *Forty Acres and a Goat*, 269, 271, 270.

Will Campbell was to write one other book of racial reconciliation, *The Stem of Jesse* (1995); its final chapter, which for the most part is a straightforward description of the integration of Mercer University in Macon, Georgia, turns into his own act of penance. At one point Campbell, who himself had played no role in earlier events at Mercer, asks, "What right do I have to tell this story? Can one person express the hurt of another?"[19] But by the end it is clear that he has become personally involved. In the last pages of the book he speaks of a ceremony held at Mercer in 1994 both in memory of Martin Luther King, Jr., and in commemoration of the integration, thirty years earlier, of the university. Campbell, invited to the two-day event, "Celebrating Our Rebirth," because he is writing a book on Mercer's integration, is called upon to speak briefly to an audience that is three-quarters black. In the crowd is Sam Oni, a Nigerian who had been the first black student at Mercer, his presence made all the more striking since the ceremony is held in a building that, in 1966, had been a church which refused Oni admission. After his graduation from Mercer, Oni had left Georgia, embittered by his experiences there.

Finding himself on the stage, at first uncertain what to say, Campbell begins to recount the ugly events that had taken place in that very building three decades earlier. Then, "by some strange, unexpected epiphany," he asks Oni to join him on the stage, and thereupon begins "some unrehearsed, unplanned verbalizing of troubled feelings":

> Mr. Oni. I am not a Mercerian. But I am white. I am Christian. I am American. A Southerner. So I was here that morning when we turned you away. I am sorry, sir, for what we did to you that day. I am sorry for what we did to ourselves. And to our God. Forgive us. (212)

After his words Campbell turns to Oni, and "a black Nigerian in his middle years, and a white Mississippian who has reached the biblical three-score years and ten, held each other in a prolonged and passionate embrace." As the crowd's applause "swept rafters once a roost of fear-become-hatred," the predominantly black assembly "took an exculpating stance." Campbell had experienced something close to racial catharsis

---

19. Campbell, *The Stem of Jesse* (Macon, Ga., 1995), 210. Hereafter cited by page number in the text.

before but not, as he describes it, this powerful or this complete: "For the first time I felt entitled, empowered, free, to tell their story" (212). To an outsider, it might have appeared a bit melodramatic, even a bit self-indulgent. But to Campbell, it was the freedom he had worked half a century to achieve.

III

FREEDOM

Willie Morris, Larry L. King, Pat Watters

In the mid-1960s, at a critical moment in the Civil Rights Movement, Robert Penn Warren produced a book titled *Who Speaks for the Negro?*, which consisted largely of Warren's interviews with African Americans south and north, among them Martin Luther King, Jr., Charles Evers, James Farmer, Bayard Rustin, James Baldwin, Ralph Ellison, Stokely Carmichael, and Malcolm X. It is somewhat similar—at least in its reliance on interviews with participants in the ongoing struggle over race in America, particularly the South—to a much more modest book, *Segregation: The Inner Conflict in the South,* Warren had written in 1956. In the earlier book Warren had, for the most part, refrained from drawing on his own racial experience—although he had concluded with a self-interview in which he asserted that racial segregation was a "moral problem" and expressed the belief that the South, if it were able "to face up to itself and its situation," might achieve "moral identity."[1] Similarly, in *Who Speaks for the Negro?* Warren largely stays out of the narrative—except, that is, for an early chapter in which he abruptly moves from the description of a black preacher in Louisiana to a memory much more personal:

> Back in the winter of 1929–30, when I was living in England, I had written an essay on the Negro in the South. I never read that essay after it was published, and the reason was, I presume, that reading it would, I dimly sensed, make me uncomfortable. In fact, while writing

1. Robert Penn Warren, *Segregation: The Inner Conflict in the South* (New York, 1956), 65–66.

it, I had experienced some vague discomfort, like the discomfort you feel when your poem doesn't quite come off, when you've had to fake, or twist, or pad it, when you haven't really explored the impulse.

The essay was a cogent and humane defense of segregation—segregation conceived of with full legal protection for the Negro, equal educational facilities, equal economic opportunities, equal pay for equal work.[2]

The essay to which Warren referred, of course, was "The Briar Patch," his contribution to the Southern Agrarian manifesto, *I'll Take My Stand* (1930), and it is true that, if he had not been exactly coerced into producing it, he was, in any case, unenthusiastic about writing it at the time. Although it "envisaged segregation" in what Warren "presumed to be its most human dimension," it was still segregation, and now, in the mid-1960s, Warren felt he had some long-overdue explaining to do. First, he did what most white southerners of noble instincts and good will, who also want to be thought well of, do: he wrote that his father had treated Negroes "right," had in the Depression refused to evict a black tenant who could not afford to pay his rent, and had not allowed anyone in his house to use "the word *nigger*" (11). The Warrens, that is, embodied *noblesse oblige,* and Warren's essay had been "very humane, self-consciously humane." But it was nonetheless a defense of segregation, and Warren had been aware at the time that "there existed a segregation that was not humane" (11). However, "it never crossed my mind that anybody could do anything about it" (12.)

In some measure, Warren never got over "The Briar Patch." Within a few years—during the Depression—he realized that he "could never again write" such an essay (12). And in the years that followed he did all he could—in his fiction, in essays, in interviews, in public addresses, and in books such as *Segregation* and *Who Speaks for the Negro?*—to make restitution. In *Who Speaks for the Negro?* he dredges up the memory of the lynching tree he saw as a child in his hometown of Guthrie, Kentucky—although "in actuality it is most improbable that I ever saw a length of rope hanging from that tree, for the lynching had taken place long before my

2. Robert Penn Warren, *Who Speaks for the Negro?* (New York, 1965), 10–11. Hereafter cited in the text by page number.

birth" (11). He recalls as well the beating of a black boy in Baton Rouge in 1939, a beating Warren first witnesses without intervening before, "in a sudden access of shame," he overcomes his paralysis and starts to move— only to be "saved" by an LSU football player who rushes in and stops the beating (13). In his book Warren cites no particular racial sins of his own— other than his hesitation to stop the 1939 beating and, even more regrettable to him, the 1930 essay, the memory of which he had carried with him for more than three decades.

Who Speaks for the Negro? was published in 1965, the same year another southern novelist, similarly expatriated to New England, published an essay in *Harper's* magazine that drew on his own earlier memories of racial transgressions. At the time he wrote the *Harper's* piece, William Styron was at work not on a conversion but rather a "confession" narrative—although the confession would be not Styron's but rather that of Nat Turner, leader of the bloody slave rebellion in Virginia in 1831. In a deeper sense, however, *The Confessions of Nat Turner* (1967) *would* be the confessions of William Styron—a book written by a white southerner, grandson of a slaveholder, speaking *as* a black southerner, a slave, at a time a century and a quarter removed from that slave's original "confession" but in a time, the 1960s, equally embroiled in racial controversy. Even if Styron's narrative had been Nat Turner's confession, it was certainly not Nat Turner's *conversion,* but it may well have been part of the process of *William Styron's* conversion—that is, an attempt on the author's part to repent of his own racial sins by not only listening to but indeed trying to get inside the skin of the black American—an attempt that, in the view of many of Styron's black critics, so misrepresented Nat that Styron was called upon to repent of the repentance.

Styron wrote his *Harper's* essay, "This Quiet Dust," to discuss his pursuit of Nat, "this Negro, who had so long occupied my thoughts, who indeed had so obsessed my imagination that he had acquired larger spirit and flesh than most of the living people I encountered day in and day out." He wrote the essay as well to deal with his own racial past, his "simple conviction" as a child that "Negroes were in every respect inferior to white people and should be made to stay in their proper order in the scheme of things." It was not that Styron's racial past was any more tainted than that of other white southerners; in fact, his father (Styron wrote elsewhere) had "done a remarkable job of shedding the racism that had been his legacy," had even become "bold enough to be a vocal advocate for tolerance and decency."[3] Still, as a child Styron's feelings about African Americans had "wobbl[ed] always between a patronizing affection . . . and downright hostility" (10). And although he makes a point of saying, as Warren had said, that the word "nigger" was not allowed in his house, he adds that "outside the confines of family . . . this was a word I commonly used" (11). Thus he was painfully aware of his own racial sins (which Styron also enumerated in essays other than this one)[4], and his search for Nat Turner was, in part, his attempt to come to terms with those sins—or, as Styron expressed it, to confront "the moral imperative of every white Southerner," which was precisely "to come to *know* the Negro." Although such an act "reek[ed] of outrageous condescension," Styron had been "haunted" (14) by the name Nat Turner ever since he learned of Turner in a Virginia history textbook, and he felt he had no choice but to seek him out and even—if in an imperfect way—give him voice.

It is no coincidence that both Styron's essay and Warren's book appeared in 1965. In the year of the Selma march and the Voting Rights Act, as well as the centenary of the end of the Civil War, the nation at last seemed stirred by a moral mandate to end, a full century later, the legacy of slavery. Never before the 1960s had there appeared to be so many white southerners of conscience, and perhaps there have not been since. Indeed, narratives of racial transformation, rare in the 1940s and 1950s, had become by the 1960s and 1970s a flourishing southern industry. Even the politicians, particularly those who had been defeated at the polls by segrega-

---

3. William Styron, "This Quiet Dust," reprinted in *"This Quiet Dust" and Other Writings* (New York, 1982), 26; and Styron, "A Horrible Little Racist," *New York Times Magazine,* 8 October 1995, p. 80. "This Quiet Dust" hereafter cited in the text by page number.

4. See, e.g., Styron, "A Horrible Little Racist" and, esp., "Jimmy in the House," reprinted in *James Baldwin: The Legacy,* ed. Quincy Troupe (New York, 1989), 43–47. In the latter essay Styron recalls the winter of 1960–61 in which James Baldwin stayed with the Styrons, living in Styron's studio. Styron remembers their long conversations, "drinking whisky through the hours until the chill dawn" (45). "Struggling still to loosen myself from the prejudices and suspicions that a southern upbringing engenders," Styron found he possessed "a residual skepticism: could a Negro *really* own a mind as subtle, as richly informed, as broadly inquiring and embracing as that of a white man?" (44–45). "My God, what appalling arrogance and vanity!" Styron, looking back, says of himself.

tionists and thus felt they had little left to lose, joined in the chorus, if only
in a minor key. Southern liberals, turned out to pasture, had long had an
honorable tradition of penning apologias of sorts, and books such as Brooks
Hays's *A Southern Moderate Speaks* (1959), Frank Smith's *Congressman
from Mississippi* (1964), Charles Longstreet Weltner's *Southerner* (1966),
and Albert Gore, Sr.'s *Let the Glory Out* (1972) were all within that high-
minded tradition. The most personal of the books was by Smith, defeated
in the 1962 congressional election largely because of his moderate stance on
race. In his book he issued "an apology for hypocrisy," expressing for the
first time "the burden of conscience that I carried without public comment
during my entire political career." Smith confesses that, "as a condition to
holding my office, I made obeisance to 'the Southern way of life.' Like the
rest of my colleagues from Mississippi and the South, I went on record with
speeches against every civil rights measure that came up during my tenure."
Yet, he writes that—despite the slaying of his deputy sheriff father by a
black man when Smith was eight years old—his views on race had always
been different from those of other white southerners: he had recognized
early the "contradiction" between Christianity and "the racial pattern in
which I was growing up." The "overriding obsession with the Negro question" in Mississippi, he believed, was "a reflection of guilt, buried in most
cases perhaps."[5]

But even Smith's book, earnest as it was, was hardly a narrative of racial

---

5. Frank Smith, *Congressman from Mississippi* (New York, 1964), vii, viii, 32, 107. In *A
Southern Moderate Speaks* (Chapel Hill, 1959), Hays, an Arkansas congressman (before
being defeated by arch-segregationist forces) as well as president of the Southern Baptist
Convention, acknowledged that as a young candidate he had been "haunted" by the faces of
African Americans in campaign crowds who would not be allowed to vote (3)—and he still
felt "deep regret" that he had done "little to help make the white leadership conscious of a
social problem at our doorstep" (11). But his regret was insufficient to keep him from trying
to justify his opposition to certain civil rights bills as well as his endorsement of the pro-
segregation Southern Manifesto in 1956. In *Southerner,* Weltner of Georgia, who earlier had
been convinced "there was no race problem" (20), writes of voting against civil rights legislation before finally taking his stand, not only voting but speaking for the Civil Rights Bill
of 1964. In 1966, after serving two terms in Congress and winning the Democratic primary
for a third term, he withdrew from the race rather than sign a state party loyalty oath that
would have required him to support Lester Maddox for governor. Gore's book was even less
a personal statement than Hays's and Weltner's.

transformation in the sense I have used the term. Despite their good intentions, politicians were so accustomed to constructing public faces that even their meditative books lacked the quality of self-exposure, of laying oneself bare, that the narratives of Lillian Smith, Boyle, Campbell, and others possessed. Such was also the case, if for different reasons, with the South's leading liberal journalists. Virginius Dabney, Jonathan Daniels, Hodding Carter, and Ralph McGill all wrote books about the South, giving a good deal of attention to race, but none of their books was a searching personal statement. Were Carter, Daniels, and Dabney incapable of such reflection? Did they not feel the burden of their own southern racial pasts? Or did they, as official southern spokesmen (particularly in an era not as given to personal expression as our own), lack the freedom to probe deeply and speak openly without jeopardizing their public positions? In any case, as expressions of the South's most celebrated racial progressives of the day, those works by Carter, Daniels, and Dabney were detached, remote, cerebral—anything but the painful and probing self-examinations of Lillian Smith, Lumpkin, Dabbs, Boyle, and Campbell.[6]

The one attempt by a prominent liberal southern journalist of that era to address race in personal terms (if one excepts, of course, W. J. Cash's *The Mind of the South,* which was, despite its pose of detachment, an intensely personal book, even a form of spiritual autobiography) was McGill's *The South and the Southerner* (1963), which had the advantage of being written several years after the books by Daniels, Dabney, and Carter and thus could partake in some manner of the new spirit of the early 1960s. But even McGill's book, if a confession of southern racial sins, is hardly a confession of

6. Daniels's *A Southerner Discovers the South* (1938) was a travel narrative, an exploration of Dixie's physical terrain rather than its heart and soul—and certainly not the author's. Dabney's *Below the Potomac* (1942) offered nothing more in the way of personal reflection. Carter's *Southern Legacy* (1950) and *Where Main Street Meets the River* (1952) provided an ideal forum for the author, located in the Mississippi Delta, to speak openly and personally about race. But other than an expression of his "warm delight" in a thirty-year friendship with a black childhood friend—who early was "companion, body servant and bodyguard" (39), then was relegated to inferior status when Carter entered college, only to benefit later from Carter's largesse—and a brief chapter titled "The Deeper Wound," in which Carter maintains that the soul of the white southerner had suffered a wound deeper than that inflicted upon the black soul, one finds almost nothing in the way of personal reflection on race.

his own. Because of his roots in the east Tennessee hills, outside the slave-holding South, McGill insists that he was "never taught any prejudice about" African Americans—a statement that is somewhat hard to accept when one considers that racial prejudice in the southern hills was often just as fierce as in the lowland South. But McGill is not hesitant to speak, on a regional level, of a troubled "conscience" and of racial "guilt." Indeed, he often echoes Lillian Smith—the object of his earlier condescension—when he speaks of racial segregation as "estrangement," as "a withdrawal from humanity that is close at hand" and of "the guilt and accusation that make up the mosaic of Southern conscience." *The South and the Southerner,* however, lacks altogether the moral voice, the passion, of Lillian Smith. Its author, after all, was the southern spokesman who had said, only a few weeks before the 1954 Supreme Court decision, "I personally hope the [Court] will not disturb segregation in the common schools."[7]

If the South's most prominent white racial liberal—a man sometimes called "the conscience of the South"—would not in the 1950s and 1960s fully probe his own conscience, and if his most prominent allies were even more reticent than he, a more obscure southern journalist, now almost entirely forgotten, was not so hesitant to probe deeply and speak frankly. In *The Wall Between* (1958), Anne Braden, a former reporter for newspapers in Birmingham and Louisville, sounded a great deal like Lillian Smith, not only in her title—which echoes Smith's emphasis on racial "walls"—and in her belief that such walls damage whites as fully as blacks, but also in her vocabulary (the "schizophrenia" of southern culture, the "sick" society of her youth, the "ugly sores" segregation "eats . . . into the soul[s] of every white person in the South") and in the description of her childhood: "I knew that something was wrong, but for years I did not understand what it was."[8] Born in Louisville in 1924 but growing up largely in Alabama and Mississippi, middle class and financially comfortable, Braden had early accepted the racial status quo. But after a time, as a "deeply religious child," she had begun to question the southern racial system, "at least sub-

7. Ralph McGill, *The South and the Southerner* (1963; reprint Athens, Ga., 1992), 64–65, 216, 218; and McGill, quoted by George McMillan, "Portrait of a Southern Liberal," *New York Review of Books,* 18 April 1974, p. 33.

8. Anne Braden, *The Wall Between* (New York, 1958), 275, 35, 226, 25. Hereafter cited in the text by page number.

consciously" (21–22), and by her late teens she had concluded that segregation was wrong. Her self-described "revelation" came not "in any blinding flash of light," but gradually as she came to see in racism a "poison" that damaged even good people like her parents—an inner poison that "contaminated their entire lives" (24). The revelation came, in part, because she took from her conservative Episcopal church in Anniston, Alabama, a lesson that seemed to be lost on its other communicants: "I . . . learned . . . that all men are brothers in God" (222). The church's influence had been "radical," after all.

Braden broke with her parents over race in her late teens, and in college in Virginia in the early 1940s she determined that she had to "challenge segregation at the roots" (26). On a trip to New York to visit a friend, she had dinner with one of the friend's acquaintances, a young black actress. Initially ill at ease—"never in my life had I eaten with a Negro"—she soon becomes caught up in their conversation and realizes "that I had completely forgotten that there was a difference in our color" (27). She responds as Katherine Lumpkin had responded to a similar recognition:

> It was a tremendous revelation. It may sound like a small thing when it is told, but it was a turning point in my life. All the cramping walls of a lifetime seemed to have come tumbling down in that moment. Some heavy shackles seemed to have fallen from my feet. For the first time in my nineteen years on this earth, I felt I had room to stretch my arms and legs and lift my head high toward the sky. . . . Here, for a moment, I glimpsed a vision of the world as it should be: where people are people, and spirits have room to grow. I never got over it. (27–28)

After Braden completes college, she goes to work on newspapers in Alabama, eventually covering the courthouse beat in Birmingham. What she experiences both contributes to her growing egalitarianism—"the concepts of 'inferior' and 'superior' began to melt away; and all that remained was people"—and to her conviction that segregation is a "curse" that must be abolished (28). Two incidents in particular confirm her belief that a kind of "death . . . gripped the South." One day a deputy sheriff leads her into a courthouse room, opens a cabinet, and takes out the skull of a black man who had been killed by a white man; the deputy lets it be known that he himself was part of the conspiracy that had allowed the murderer to go free. Even more distressing than the hideous skull—which "filled the room and the world" and left Braden "terror-stricken" (29)—is an event that makes Braden realize that, despite her resolve, she herself is part of an "evil" that "winds itself about your soul like the arms of an octopus" (30). One morning at breakfast in a Birmingham cafeteria, after calling the sheriff's office to check on the previous night's activities, she responds to a friend's question "Anything doing?" with the words "Everything quiet. Nothing but a colored murder." ("No'm, killed a nigger," Huck had said when asked if anyone had been hurt in a steamboat accident—to which his questioner replied, "It's lucky . . . sometimes people do get hurt.")[9] Braden might not have realized what she had said if she had not sensed the stiffness—the "stony mask"—of a black woman who was at that moment pouring them coffee. Filled with remorse, she cannot, however, take back her words. She too, she realizes, is still "a part of this white world that considered a Negro life not worth bothering about" (30–31).

Not long afterward—finding herself "strangled . . . want[ing] air . . . want[ing] freedom," feeling she has "to escape from the social decay and the death symbolized by [the] skull" (31–32)—Braden leaves Birmingham for a job on the Louisville *Times*. Later, she and her husband—whom she had met at the *Times*—leave the newspaper to work with Louisville trade unions, the NAACP, and other interracial groups. Becoming a self-professed "radical" in the early 1950s, driven to change the racial status quo "before any more children grew up absorbing the poison I had absorbed," she finds that striking out "against segregation became like a compulsion to me" (34). It is her single-mindedness, at least as unwavering as Lillian Smith's, that leads to Braden's involvement in racial conflict in Louisville, brings her anonymous phone calls, death threats, a midnight visit by a white mob, and finally sends her to jail. Her primary offense is joining with her husband in 1954 to buy a house in a white neighborhood and then immediately deeding that house to a black friend who, because of racial restrictions, could not have bought it from the original sellers. In the eyes of white Louisville—which, only one week later, would be inflamed by the Supreme Court decision outlawing school segregation—Braden and her husband had gone too far.

9. Mark Twain, *Adventures of Huckleberry Finn*, 207.

Most of the rest of Braden's book describes the price she and her husband pay for their racial apostasy: between 1954 and 1957 they fall victim to an unholy alliance of red-baiters and segregationists. After the house, occupied by their black friend and his wife, is bombed and half-destroyed, Braden and her husband are falsely charged with "conspiracy" in the bombing—they are alleged to have done it to stir up racial trouble. After their own house is raided and books by Marx and Lenin and other Communist writers are found, they are indicted for sedition, and Braden's husband is convicted. Finally, seven months into Carl Braden's fifteen-year sentence, his conviction is overturned, the indictment against her is thrown out, and the racial furor subsides. But even as she writes in 1958, Braden has not retreated from the struggle for racial justice. Indeed she, as fully as any racially awakened southerner, recognizes the nature of racial conversion: "Race prejudice being an emotional thing cannot be removed by intellectual arguments alone. There must be some real emotional experience" (51). "The throbbing of [her] conscience" (35) had driven her to do what she felt she had to do.

After she wrote *The Wall Between,* Anne Braden descended into an obscurity nearly as deep as that from which she had come. Continuing to live in Louisville, she threw herself into the work of that refuge of earlier southern radicals, the Southern Conference Educational Fund, but she wrote no more books of note. Her book had been, in every sense, a product of those racially charged times of the 1950s, a period that had a similar effect on a number of other, more prominent (or soon to be so) southern journalists, also born in the 1920s and 1930s, who came of age, intellectually and morally, at midcentury and who responded to those troubled times in a similar fashion, by probing their own consciences (if, often, unlike Braden, after crossing the Potomac and Ohio, heading north) and producing narratives of racial transformation—journalists more independent and less burdened by institutional responsibilities than Ralph McGill and Hodding Carter, and figures who, if geographically detached from the South as they wrote, were hardly emotionally detached. The most prominent of those was perhaps Willie Morris, wunderkind of sixties literary journalism, who assumed the editorship of *Harper's* in 1967, at the age of thirty-three. A Mississippian by way of the University of Texas, Oxford, and the *Texas Observer,* Morris came to New York in 1963 to work for *Harper's,* and four years later he had ascended to its pinnacle. He had brought with him an Oxford degree, a great deal of knowledge about Texas politics, a winning prose style, and a love-hate relationship with his native state reminiscent of those love-hate affairs of certain of Faulkner's fictional Mississippians. In his most notable book, *North Toward Home,* written in New York in the mid-sixties, Morris explores that relationship.

Morris's memoir is less exclusively about race than those works by Smith, Lumpkin, Dabbs, Boyle, Campbell, and Braden. But race nonetheless is at the center of his quarrel with his homeland, and his book is equally a narrative of racial transformation. In its pages he paints an essentially cheerful picture of his youth in Yazoo City, Mississippi, in the 1940s and early 1950s. Morris's father was a Tennessean who had come south to work for Cities Service gasoline, but Morris's mother's family had deep roots in Mississippi—an ancestor had been acting territorial governor in the early nineteenth century—and Willie Morris himself was securely fixed in place. In the early chapters of *North Toward Home,* he describes a boyhood worthy of Tom Sawyer, playing pranks, roaming the river town with his pals and his dog, playing baseball. Religion to him was not always the gravely serious matter it was to Lillian Smith, James McBride Dabbs, and Will Campbell; but it was, among other things, such an exciting affair that before he turned twelve, he writes, "I had been 'saved,' not once, but at least a dozen times."[10] And it was serious enough that the influence of his Methodist upbringing never fully left him, thus when he went on to Austin, Oxford, and New York he always felt a certain vacuum: "The preachers, the revivals, the prayers, and especially the good old hymns my mother would play on the organ in the church—these are still so real to me that when I hear church bells on some lonely, cold Sunday morning on Manhattan Island, I feel a touch of guilt, and the remorseless pull of my precocious piety" (55).

"The town in which I had grown up had yet to be touched by the great television culture," Morris writes in *North Toward Home.* "Something was

10. Willie Morris, *North Toward Home* (1967; reprint, Oxford, Miss., 1982), 38. Hereafter cited in the text by page number.

left, if but an oblique recollection: a Southern driftlessness, a closeness to the earth, a sense of time standing still, a lingering isolation from America's relentless currents of change and homogeneity. Something else also remained, some innocent and exposed quality that made possible, in the heart of a young and vulnerable boy, an allegiance and a love for a small, inconsequential place" (142). That place, half black and half white, included what Morris as a child felt to be racial harmony. He and his parents were kind to blacks, and they were kind to him; when Morris was not yet a year old, his life had been saved by a black doctor when a white doctor could not be found. Morris played football with black boys, and when he and his friends encountered them on the street, "there would be bantering, half-affectionate exchanges" (82). Indeed, the young Morris felt there was a certain mystique about being black: "There was a stage, when we were about thirteen, in which we 'went Negro.' We tried to broaden our accents to sound like Negroes. . . . We consciously walked like young Negroes, mocking their swinging gait" (81). And "the ineluctable attraction of nigger-town" included as well "Negro girls and women [who] were a source of constant excitement and sexual feeling for me, and filled my day-dreams with delights and wonders" (79).

But there was another side to small-town race relations that Morris recognized even then, "a boy's recurring sense impressions of a hovering violence, isolated acts that remained in my memory long afterward, as senseless and unpatterned later as they had been for me when they happened" (87). Even as a very young child he had sensed something was wrong. When he crossed the street to play with black children, his mother "came and got me and yanked me home": "Don't ever play back here again. . . . Just you don't" (17–18). As he grew older, Morris found himself playing cruel jokes on African Americans young and old:

We would hide in the hedges in my back yard and shoot Negro men who were walking down the sidewalk, aiming BB's at their tails. We would throw dead snakes from the trees into their path, or dead rats and crawfish, or attach a long thread to a dollar bill on the sidewalk and, when the man stopped to pick it up, pull it slowly back into the bushes.

I took to phoning the Negro undertakers, talking in my flawless Negro accent. (84)

On another occasion, when he was twelve, Morris recalls "lurking in the bushes" (a curious turn of phrase, usually associated in white southern mythology with feared *black* perpetrators of violence), waiting for a little black boy—who "could not have been more than three"—as he walked along with his older sister. When the boy "got in front of me . . . I jumped out and pounced upon him. I slapped him across the face, kicked him with my knee, and with a shove sent him sprawling on the concrete." As the boy's sister shouted "What'd he *do* to you?" Morris's heart beat "furiously, in terror and a curious pleasure" (77).

Later, Morris writes, it seemed as if his actions and those of his friends took on an even more "specific edge of cruelty":

> On Canal Street, across from the old Greyhound station at the Bayou, there was a concrete bannister where the Negroes would sit waiting for the busses. On Saturday nights we would cruise down the street in a car, and the driver would open his door and drive close to the curb. We would watch while the Negroes, to avoid the car door, toppled backward off the bannister like dominoes. And the taunts and threats to the isolated Negroes we saw, on country roads and deserted white streets, were harder and more cruel than anything we had done as children. (89–90)

Morris later repents of his "unthinking sadism" (90), but the memory of his offenses stays with him. Later, in New York, when he accidentally bumps a black man on the subway and the man "sneer[s]" at him, remarking on Morris's "cracker accent" and his origins in the Mississippi "mud" (347–48), it is *Morris,* the innocent in this case, who comes away from the encounter feeling guilty.

If Morris conforms to the racial conversion narrative in the confession of his racial sins, he does not, as Smith, Boyle, and Campbell, identify one great moment of awakening, a time when the magnitude of all those sins becomes clear. The moment that comes closest to such an awakening is upon his return to Yazoo City in the summer of 1955, just before his senior year at the University of Texas. Going to Texas in the first place had been a move toward a "liberality of spirit, an *expansiveness*" (152–53), undertaken at age eighteen after his father had advised him to "get the hell out of Mississippi" (140)—although at the time Morris was not sure why his father had said that. He still did not understand altogether as he drove, in 1955, back from Texas into the early Mississippi summer: "the very air was pervaded with an odor so fragrant as to make the senses reel with a wonderful anticipation and longing. . . . I had the most overwhelming sense of coming *home,* to some place that belonged to me; I was not merely stunned by its beauty . . . I was surprised to feel so settled inside, as if nothing, no matter how cruel and despairing, could destroy my belonging" (176–77).

What Morris was to find in Yazoo City on this occasion would change that feeling forever. On the third or fourth day of his visit, he heard rumblings about a "meeting" to be held in the school auditorium; the purpose of the meeting, he learned from a friend, was to organize a chapter of the White Citizens Council, in response to the 1954 Supreme Court decision and, in particular, to an NAACP petition signed by fifty-three local black parents seeking an immediate end to school segregation. Morris went with his friend to the meeting, called by "sixteen of the most prominent white men in town," and what he found in the packed auditorium that night, with its atmosphere of "claustrophobic terror," its foot-stomping, and its shouts of "Let's get them *niggers!*" (177–78), seems a twentieth-century southern version of what Hawthorne's Young Goodman Brown found when he happened upon the good Puritans of Salem Village in depths of Satan's forest: "On the stage, sitting in straight-back chairs, were just over a dozen men. I knew them all; some of them were fathers of my best friends, men I had known and admired and could talk to on a first-name basis. In the audience were scores of men and women I had known as far back as my childhood. I saw my father there, sitting next to one of our neighbors" (178). When the meeting began, the chairman proposed "steps to be taken" to punish the signers of the petition: they would be fired from their jobs, evicted from their rental homes, refused groceries by white grocers. When a neighbor of Morris's rises to point out that such actions were unconstitutional, he is "abruptly drowned out by the roar from the crowd" and subjected to "boos and catcalls that might have wilted Judge Earl Warren himself" (179). As for Morris, who had only a few days earlier felt that "nothing, no matter how cruel and despairing" (176), could destroy his "belonging" to his town:

> I sat there, quiet as could be. For a brief moment I was tempted to
> stand up and support my neighbor, but I lacked the elemental cour-

age to go against that mob. For it *was* a mob, and I was not the same person I had been three years before. In the pit of my stomach, I felt a strange and terrible disgust. I looked back and saw my father, sitting still and gazing straight ahead; on the stage my friends' fathers nodded their heads and talked among themselves. I felt an urge to get out of there. *Who are these people?* I asked myself. What was I doing there? Was this the place I had grown up in and never wanted to leave? I knew in that instant, in the middle of a mob in our school auditorium, that a mere three years in Texas had taken me irrevocably, even without my recognizing it, from home. (179–80)

If Morris had a single racial epiphany, that was it. He returned to Texas, then came back to Yazoo City later that year—after the black signers of the petition had indeed been fired and otherwise economically punished—and (in a story Morris relates not in *North Toward Home* but in a later book) he told the assembled members of the Rotary Club, as their invited speaker, that, "for the sake of preserving the broad essentials of the society they wanted to keep," they should integrate the schools immediately. Otherwise, "they would have a revolution in Yazoo someday." When two or three leading townsmen came up to Morris afterward, "trembling in rage, saying . . . that I was advocating heresy if not bloodshed," Morris realized that his own attempts as racial prophet were futile. Although he did not believe (as his future wife was to believe) that Mississippi was "elementally evil . . . a symbol of all that was wrong with all of us,"[11] he knew that he had willed himself out of a community that he had once loved.

As he writes *North Toward Home*, Morris sits in his Upper West Side apartment, just prior to becoming editor-in-chief of *Harper's*. It is now more than a decade later and, racially speaking, he is now a self-proclaimed "converted Southern boy" (378). He has become friends with the African American writers Ralph Ellison and Al Murray, and with Ellison in particular he feels a bond: "We shared the same easygoing conversation; the casual talk and the telling of stories, in the Southern verbal jam-session way; the sense of family and the past and people out of the past; the congenial social manner and the mischievous laughter" (384). Ellison, he insists, helped him come to terms with his shame over his Mississippi origins: "shame was

11. Willie Morris, *Yazoo*, 18, 19, 25–26.

too simple and debilitating an emotion, too easy and predictable—like bitterness. It was more difficult to *understand* one's origins" (386). He, Ellison, and Murray even celebrate their southern roots, gathering at Murray's Harlem apartment on New Year's Day 1967 for ham-hocks, black-eyed peas, collard greens, cornbread, and bourbon. It was, Morris writes, "a kind of ritual for all of us" (387), and also a ritual in a sense he may not have intended, a sacramental partaking of the elements of racial reconciliation—soul food in more ways than one.

Morris concludes *North Toward Home* with the description of a trip in October 1965 from New York back to Texas, where he gives a speech, and to Mississippi, where he visits his mother and grandmother. He brings along his five-year-old son. He stays in Yazoo City, in his boyhood home, only one night, and the next morning he rises early and drives around the town with his mother. He is "suffused with a physical feeling of lost things, with a tangible hovering presence of old dead moments," but he also realizes "it was time to get out," and he drives as fast as he can for Jackson and the airport. Along the highway he sees a "huge billboard" with "a picture of Martin Luther King, surrounded by throngs of Negroes," and the words on the sign say "M.L. King Meets His Fellow Commies" (435). Most of the memories Morris has as they drive into Jackson, however, are not unpleasant ones—he sees his grandfather's old house, another ancestral house, and a cemetery in which ancestors lie—but by the time he and his son reach the airport, his thoughts are on other things. "Why was it," he asks, "in such moments just before I leave the South, did I always feel some easing of a great burden?" It was as if "someone had taken some terrible weight off my shoulders, or as if some old grievance had suddenly fallen away." With such questions Morris boards the plane, takes off, circles the city, and turns "north toward home" (437–38).

Such is the conclusion of *North Toward Home,* but such is hardly the end of the story of Willie Morris and the South. He was to return to Yazoo City in 1970—somewhat apprehensive since his book "had deeply disturbed the town"—to write another book, *Yazoo* (1971), about the successful integration of his old high school. He was also to write another book of memories, almost all pleasant this time, of his Delta boyhood, this book penance perhaps for the earlier penance that had been *North Toward Home.* He was to write other essays on home, some sliding into the sentimental, and in

1980 he was to come home for good, not to harsh criticism, as southern racial converts and truth-tellers traditionally had, but to honors and rewards,
as writer in residence at the University of Mississippi. Continuing the saga
of his life, somewhat in the fashion of his early idol Thomas Wolfe (except
that Morris, in his autobiographical works, didn't *pretend* to write fiction),
he would in his later book of memoirs, *New York Days* (1993), offer some
reasons for his return to "the sweet and deep dark womb of home." One of
the reasons, unstated, was simply that the overriding theme of all Morris's
work, like Wolfe's, was a search for home; like Wolfe's, the titles of Morris's
books—not only *North Toward Home* but also *Homecomings* and *"Terrains
of the Heart" and Other Essays on Home*—demonstrate that fact. But there
were other reasons for his return of which Morris himself was quite aware.
As he acknowledges, "The external juxtaposition of my state's hate and
love, the apposition of its severity and tenderness, would forever baffle and
enrage me, but perhaps that is what I needed all along."[12] The craftsman of
his own life's story that Morris had become, recognizing the need to bring
things full circle—or was it just the sentimentalist in him?—led him to
give to the final chapter of his New York book the title "South Toward
Home." And from the 1980s on, he would indeed continue to live in Mississippi.

Willie Morris, during his editorship of *Harper's* from 1967 to 1971, not
only continued to write about the South, and often in the pages of his own
magazine; he also provided a forum for Robert Penn Warren, William
Styron, Walker Percy, James Dickey, Truman Capote, Marshall Frady,
Maya Angelou, Bill Moyers, and numerous other southerners, resident and

---

12. Willie Morris, *"Terrains of the Heart" and Other Essays on Home* (Oxford, Miss.,
1981), 63; and Morris, *New York Days* (Boston, 1993), 368. In a much later book, *The
Ghosts of Medgar Evers* (New York, 1998)—a book largely about the making and reception
of the film *Ghosts of Mississippi*—Morris again writes of his depth of feeling for Mississippi,
his "love and fear" of the Delta in particular. In this book Morris repeats the story he had
told in *North Toward Home,* of whites driving by the bus station, opening car doors, and
toppling blacks who were sitting on a concrete bannister waiting for busses. In *North
Toward Home* he had said he was involved in such activity; here he assigns the cruelty to
others.

expatriate, to tell about the South in its pages. In September 1967 Styron published a 45,000-word excerpt of his forthcoming novel *The Confessions of Nat Turner* in *Harper's*. Indeed, for a time during Morris's tenure at the magazine, it seemed that every other issue carried a piece entitled "New Orleans Mon Amour" or "Memphis" or "Going Home to Raleigh" or "The Grand Ole Opry" or "The Vision from Hilton Head." One of these essays, Larry L. King's meditation on racial guilt in January 1970, was the beginning of what would become one of the most notable of post–Civil Rights Movement racial conversion narratives, King's *Confessions of a White Racist* (1971).

Larry King came to racial conversion, however, in a manner somewhat different from Lillian Smith, James McBride Dabbs, and the other racial converts I have discussed—not through religion (since, at least by his teens, he had little), nor through some extension of *noblesse oblige* (that, his family didn't have either), nor even through early residence in the traditional South. King was born in 1929 in Putnam, Texas—a land far more western than southern—and he grew up largely in west Texas, the son of a family of no great distinction or historical consciousness or social or economic standing. In fact, the Kings, if not actually poor, were of very modest means. King's father farmed for a time, then held a series of jobs, including construction worker and night watchman for an oil company for about a dollar an hour—a position that led King to label himself "the night watchman's son."[13] Nor did the young King have any driving ambition; he was interested mostly in playing football and in whatever good times a Texas boyhood could bring. He finished high school in Texas, joined the army, went for a year of college at Texas Tech, and worked for a couple of southwestern newspapers. Then, hitching his unpromising star to a Texas congressman, he went to Washington in 1954, and in the years that followed, just before and during the Johnson administration, he gained a certain cachet, as many country-smart and colorful Texans did during that era. If one was a poor boy from the provinces, it helped to be what was called a character—and King (not unlike, in another setting, another poor country boy, Will Campbell) was adjudged to be precisely that. By the time Willie Morris met

13. Larry L. King, *Confessions of a White Racist* (New York, 1971), 21. Hereafter cited in the text by page number.

King in the mid-1960s he was already a "flamboyant and outspoken" figure with a "hardy and questing eye." He was also on his way to becoming a highly successful writer and playwright, the author of *The Best Little Whorehouse in Texas,* which, as Morris has remarked, "allowed him to purchase a mansion in Washington, hire nannies for his children, and subsidize their riding lessons in Virginia." "What," Morris exclaimed, "would his old West Texas daddy say?"[14]

But King was hardly a success at first, not when he sat down in 1969 to write his *Confessions.* It was a time when King was preoccupied with race, as he felt any other American with social antennae should have been in the years just after the Civil Rights Movement, after the assassination of Martin Luther King, Jr., widespread riots in American cities, and a resulting suspicion, if not hostility, between blacks and whites. As King writes in his introduction, his "is a not a book about black Americans so much as one about white Americans and their racist attitudes." Further,

> It is not my individual confession alone, but a gratuitous admission of guilt on behalf of all white racists past and present, malignant or benign. It is not, I think (once the reader permits this opening oratory), a strident moral preachment so much as a journey of one white American who, boy and man, goes wandering through his time and his country. Sometimes he is blind; occasionally he sees. And always his journey is made easier by the color of his skin. (ix)

14. Morris, *New York Days,* 374. A decade before King wrote, another white Texan, John Howard Griffin, had written *Black Like Me* (1961), which had gained far more attention than King's book was to; Griffin's sold more than three million copies. The story of Griffin's trip through the South as a "black man"—or, rather, a man with chemically-changed skin who passed for black—Griffin's book was in no measure a conversion narrative. His racial transformation had occurred earlier, during a period of blindness that lasted from 1947 until 1957, at which time surgery restored his sight. As he tells the story to John Egerton (in *A Mind to Stay Here,* 146–60), Griffin had already begun to question his heritage of racism before he suffered the wound in World War II that led to his blindness, but it was the total blindness that changed him altogether—simply because "as a blind man I couldn't tell black from white" (150). In a curious manner, then, Griffin reverses the assumption of other white racial converts who use blindness metaphorically: he never sees so clearly until he *becomes* blind. In other respects he sounds a great deal like Lillian Smith and James McBride Dabbs—in his emphasis on the "sickness" and "evil" of a racist South and his belief that "our humanity is being saved by black people" (158).

King writes, then, as a racial convert (although one still "sometimes . . . blind"), and he is overwhelmed by a sense of individual and national guilt:

> If today one could magically concoct a single white man and fairly charge him, as an individual, with all the racist crimes of America against one theoretical black man representative of his people's many victimizations, I am convinced, no jury in love with justice would have any recourse other than to hang him high, with the recommendation that he be permitted to strangle by fractions. To vote for Whitey's acquittal, our hypothetical jurors would find it necessary to ignore three hundred years of chicanery including kidnaping, slavery, broken family units and shattered promises, racial segregation with its debilitating humiliations . . . and, incredibly, murder by mob rule more than five thousand times within the first forty years of the twentieth century alone. Someone else must rise for the defense. I haven't any. This white man's burden is, simply, the white man's history. (xi)

King speaks, then, as a representative white American, but he also speaks as an individual, "forty-two, a veteran observer of racist America" (x), who "may have thought more on the subject of racism, and for longer" and may "have even come a longer way than most" (ix). He realizes as well the price of his confession. He knows "that some old friends, relatives, or associates will recognize themselves in so personal a recitation, no matter what beards I put them behind, and will be offended or hurt or both." Such was, King adds, "particularly likely to be true of members of my immediate family, who are perhaps too clearly identified (and seemingly too summarily judged) to make either them or the author comfortable with the results." "Some of the people" King loves most "harbor their own disapproving opinions of my racial views, just as this book perhaps all too clearly reveals my disagreement with their attitudes" (xviii).

In the first chapter of his *Confessions,* King discusses his own early racial history—which is not nearly so rich and full as the histories of Lillian Smith, Lumpkin, and other eventual racial converts. Since his little west Texas town of Putnam "discouraged Negro residents," and the town of Cisco where his family later lived had only a few more African Americans, his childhood racial memories were sparse—a few old black men shuffling along the streets of south Cisco, smiling obsequiously, a black shoeshine

boy who was the butt of "rough country humor," and blacks in grocery stores "step[ping] back to permit white customers easy access to the
vegetable bins or to the single check-out counter" (8). Many of King's early
racial impressions, in fact, came from a distance—from Amos and Andy
radio broadcasts; from a minstrel show that came to town, with Rastus and
Sambo in cork-blackened faces; from hearing the broadcast of Joe Louis's
1937 knockout of Jimmy Braddock for the world heavyweight championship. Indeed, "each time Joe Louis fought, the farmers of our community
and their sons gathered before a common old battery-operated radio in the
unifying prayer that some 'white hope' would whip ole Joe's black ass for
us" (7)—this at the same time that scores of rural southern blacks were
gathering around *their* radios praying just the opposite. From all these
fleeting impressions—"quite without knowing how I came by the gift, and
in a complete absence of even the slightest contact with black people"—
King assimilated "certain absolutes":

> The Negro would steal anything lying around loose and a high per
> centage of all that was bolted down; you couldn't hurt him if you hit
> him on the head with a tire tool; he revered watermelon above all
> other fruits of the vine; he had a mule's determination not to work
> unless driven or led to it; he would screw a snake if somebody would
> hold its head. (6)

When King's family moved, in his teens, to the oil town of Midland, he
encountered both African Americans and the world of Jim Crow as he
never had before, although neither made much of an impression on him at
the time. He saw blacks being herded into the balcony of the movie theater,
he saw signs for "White" and "Colored" waiting rooms at the train depot,
and signs at the front of restaurants announcing that their proprietors reserved the right to refuse service to anyone they chose. It hardly occurred to
him that human dignity was a casualty of such restrictions. But he was
aware, even then, of curious intersections of race, class, and religion—in
particular, was aware that "some of the more obvious white-supremacy advocates of my youth were men of the cloth" (18). Though "by the time [he]
reached puberty," King remarked elsewhere, he was persuaded to attend
church "only by shouts and main force," his parents were so given to old-
time religion that King's mother had once hoped he would become a

preacher.[15] His father, in fact, was himself an occasional country preacher "without the benefit of formal training or official sanction, though he had in his sixteenth year quite clearly heard the Call while working one hot day in a cornfield" (18). Thus in King's formative years his home was "fair game for a series of trembling itinerant prophets who, upon completing a wild pulpit-pounding sermon only thirty minutes shorter than the Fundamentalist concept of Eternity's promises or threats," came to the Kings for fried chicken and further declaiming on the Virgin Birth and "how the earth was most assuredly flat." But that was not all on which these "unlettered priests" held forth: another of their favorite topics was "the vast amount of Scriptural authority accounting for the black man's lowly state and substandard conduct" (18).

King's first racial crisis—one he met with something less than distinction—occurred when, as a part-time mailman at age sixteen, he refused to train a black war veteran the Midland Post Office had hired because of a manpower shortage. "Well, hell . . . he's a *nigger*," King had given as sufficient reason for his refusal, then added that he would be ashamed if his friends saw him with the black man. He reconsiders only because he will lose his own job if he doesn't comply with the postmaster's order. The morning his new duties are scheduled to begin, King arrives at work, shakes hands with the new employee—the first time he "had suffered such an intimacy with a black man" (22)—and heads out on his route apprehensively. The night watchman's son—embarrassed "when we encountered my classmates while walking in affluent neighborhoods"—is polite but formal to his charge: "The day Tim was assigned his own route was a happy one for me" (23). Taking no moral instruction from his two-week adventure in integration, King resolves instead to stay away from Negroes. When he finishes high school in 1946, he chooses the navy over other branches of service because "it was said to admit fewer blacks" (24). Failing the navy's visual test, he is forced to join the army after all—and is brought, unwillingly, to his racial awakening.

What he hears at first of black soldiers—from members of his all-white unit—reinforces his early prejudices: African Americans in World War II, he was told, were cowards in combat, "deserted in droves and generally

15. Larry L. King, *None But a Blockhead: On Being a Writer* (New York, 1986), 5–6.

were not worth the shot it took to kill them." They also sought "to ingratiate themselves with European women" (35). King does all he can to uphold what W. J. Cash had called "the proto-Dorian bond," or white racial solidarity: at basic training in New Jersey, when two black men come in and sit beside him at a lunch counter, he eats "in a choked and humble silence"— and then creates the fiction, in a letter to his parents, that he and his friends had "cleared [them] out in a hurry" (36). Since President Truman's order desegregating the armed forces was almost two years away, King at first had little contact with black soldiers. When, at Fort Monmouth, New Jersey, he did come face to face with his first African American officer, he "felt a moment of panic while old prejudices struggled with newly acquired military disciplines." Then King "snapped him a proper salute" (37).

King's racial awakening, thus, was a gradual one—and all the more so since, in some respects, he had to go through all the racial stages a white youth, born in the heart or at least on the close fringes of Dixie, had undergone in early years. He had to come to *know* blacks on some basis, if only a paternalistic one, a goal he accomplishes when he makes the acquaintance of a good-natured cook from Alabama, "a good goddamn nigger" who makes the white soldiers laugh. King falls into the habit of sitting on the cook's footlocker, drinking with him, and listening to his tales. Gradually King comes to realize that "Brewster was brighter than most people I had known, more complex, full of more hidden secrets and silent victories." Although it bothers King "as being against the Lord's intent," he "continued to sit at [the cook's] feet" (37–38). One night, finding himself drinking from the same bottle as the cook—"not bothering to wipe the neck off, and feeling a little noble and extremely daring"—he asks Brewster what it is like to be a black man in a white outfit. "It's all right," the cook answers. "If you ain't got no pride." (38). Then, King observes, "after a few throbbing seconds of silence he burst into laughter." (38).

But King is not to experience his first total immersion in racial integration until, a few months later, he is assigned to a base on Long Island where black soldiers are "methodically assimilated: to sit with us at table, sleep alongside us, and be assigned to jobs without regard to color" (39). Serving as administrative aide to the company commander, King works closely with a black first sergeant from rural Georgia, with whom his relationship is "proper and generally easy" and whom he comes to consider, at the time, a "close friend" (40). Only twenty years later, in writing his *Confessions,* does King realize they had not been close at all: although they had eaten together in the mess hall and had listened to baseball games together, never did the sergeant invite King to his off-base apartment and never did they go out on the town together. But at least, King felt, he treated the sergeant with a certain respect—unlike his unwitting treatment of another black man, who, during King's brief stay in the base hospital, swept and mopped his room and attended to his needs in a manner that went beyond, King felt, the call of duty. Wondering why the black private was so attentive to him, King asks the man—who has said such service is "part of [his] life's work"—if he had been a porter in civilian life. "No," responds the private. "I was a student in a seminary, studying to become a minister. I've had three years of college." Experiencing an early pang of racial guilt, King reports, "He never came back" (43).

In fact, King's racial education takes place off base as much as on, and for reasons at first only tangentially concerned with race. If he had been assigned to a southern military camp, his off-base education might not have been so beneficial. But spending a great deal of his free time in Manhattan, he comes to know an aspiring actress, who introduces him to Greenwich Village and "my first show folk, struggling authors, lesbians, marijuana experiments, and revolutionary dialogue" (53). Although the bohemian crowd to which King becomes attached is "more democratic than most in its racial attitudes" (55)—and he adjusts his own attitudes accordingly—he is not prepared to accept some of what he sees. He is not shocked by interracial couples if the couple consists of a white man and a black woman, but when he sees a black man with a white woman he finds himself reacting strangely: "Inside my white boy's craw I was resentful, fearful, perhaps a little sickened" (55).

By the time he leaves the army in mid-1949, however, King considers himself racially liberated—at least in relation to his fellow white Americans. Returning to Texas and enrolling as a freshman at Texas Tech in Lubbock, where "not a single black face" is to be seen (61), he takes stock:

Though my racial experiences in the Army and in the East had been less complete than I had presumed, exposure to black people at least had taught me that they had minds, dreams, and hurts like the rest of

us, and in no way deserved their automatic exclusion. It wasn't so
much seeing the black citizen without social or economic opportunity, or confined to his slums and inferior schools—though, God
knows, these were major causes of our terrible social impasse. No, it
was the million mindless "little" humiliations that stirred my tardy
rage and soon caused me to be looked on as a little crazy and
unreliable. (68)

Actually, King rather relishes the role of "crazy and unreliable" iconoclast,
speaking up in public gatherings and shocking people with his views on
race. He has decided by this time that he wants to be writer, and has concluded that detachment from the herd seems to be his natural state. He has
run-ins over race with his father, whom he now calls a racist peckerwood,
and, after he drops out of Texas Tech, run-ins with editors on the newspapers on which he works. Like Willie Morris, he has willed himself out of the
community in which he had once felt so secure, but unlike Morris—who
can return to Austin and then to Oxford—for a time King has nowhere else
to go.

When King does manage a way out of Texas in late 1954, as a congressional assistant, he expects to find in Washington, D.C., a model of racial
democracy. What he finds instead is a city with unequal opportunities, unequal housing (he himself is refused an apartment over the phone because,
he learns later, his southern accent is mistaken for black), and congressmen
who vote for civil rights legislation and tell racist jokes. Although King considers himself a racial convert, he is not immune to backsliding. Indeed, he
numbers himself among those "well-fed white liberals who sat in our sub-
urban homes congratulating ourselves and mankind on the passage of tame
civil rights bills, or cheering edicts by the Warren court" but who "were pa-
thetically tardy in understanding that such actions were of small moment in
the absence of enthusiastic enforcement at all levels of government" (112).
And when the Freedom Riders rolled South in 1961 and King "was
moved" to join them, "neither my Congressman nor my former wife had
difficulty persuading me against that course, by citing dangers to my political sponsor, to my family, or to my physical person" (113).

The remainder of King's *Confessions* consists largely of racial regrets and
disillusionment. For a time he entertains hope, particularly as he finds him-

self caught up in the spirit of Martin Luther King, Jr.'s speech during the 1963 March on Washington. "We thrilled to that dream," Larry King writes, "and to the fantastically huge, orderly, singing, loving crowd of all shades and hues, backgrounds and heritages, opportunities and privations" (129). But the urban riots in the summer of 1965—"something more" than riots, he felt, "an insurrection, a revolt, a revolution"—put an end to that dream: "So blind was most of white America to ghetto conditions, so isolated and protected from the realities of the black slums, that we failed to realize how little even of their own squalor black people owned" (141). King's pattern of hope and then disillusionment plays itself out several other times. He tires of Washington and begins to frequent New York literary circles, expecting—as he had expected when he came to Washington—to find racial enlightenment but finding instead another form of white racism. Later, in 1969, he goes to Harvard as a Nieman Fellow, expecting a respite from racial tensions; what he finds instead is racism, now both white and black. When a young black man at a party learns that King is writing a book to be entitled *Confessions of a White Racist*, he "sneered and berated me for my exploitations" (156).

King should have expected as much, particularly in the racial climate of 1969. A confession of white racial sins did seem rather self-indulgent, after all. Who was to benefit from such a confession, an angry African American might have asked. Certainly not American blacks. But, King believed, it was all he *could* do, given all that had gone before—that and his occasional "bleeding-heart good deed or two"—and his helplessness, finally, was the source of his frustration. Further, he found himself, after the riots of the mid- and late 1960s, becoming "sorely afraid of the black man" (146). He has a run-in with a black street gang in Washington, he has rocks thrown at him by another group of young black boys, he encounters rudeness in stores and on the streets. He understands *why,* but still he rues the fact that "where I had once walked the streets in confidence, I came to look ahead like a soldier advancing into enemy territory, alert for unfriendly blacks or side-street dangers, vulnerable, tense, and marked—at last—by my white skin" (147). As Washington burns, in the wake of Martin Luther King's murder in 1968, Larry King finds himself cowering behind his door, looking through the peephole at two well-dressed black men and deciding, "for safety's sake," not to answer, while one of the men makes jokes about

"Whitey being afraid to come out of his hole." That night, hearing gun-shots and the sounds of sirens in his neighborhood, King sleeps "with a billy club fashioned from a broomstick and a wicked butcher knife next to [his] bed" (149).

As King concludes his book, in September 1970, his outlook is alto-gether bleak. For him, as for Sarah Patton Boyle, the Civil Rights Move-ment had been about much more than school integration, voting rights, and black access to public accommodations; it had also been about a spirit of interracial cooperation that he once had glimpsed but now feels—as Boyle had felt ten years earlier, with less reason—has disappeared. He un-derstands the reasons for the new black militancy, but he deeply regrets it all the same. And he has no choice but to count himself, at least in spirit, among those white liberals who, fewer than ten years before, had marched and sung for black freedom but who now "tend to feel betrayed and sorry for themselves now that a large part of the black community rejects them": "All that integrated praying, hand-clapping, and hymn-singing of yesterday having failed to purify the national heart, the black man wants no more." The black American, rather, wants "black separatism, black control of black destinies, black institutions for black people . . . black power. And it scares us to death" (166).

The despair in King's tone in his final pages is unmistakable. Racial con-fession—and conversion—was not supposed to end this way. He had rec-ognized his sins, he had repented, he had been transformed, but now it ap-pears that his own racial sins, and those of his white countrymen, had been too great to be forgiven after all—forgiven, that is, by those against whom the sins had been committed. Perhaps that was the trouble with secular conversion all along. "Increasingly," King concludes, "I am judged by blacks as arbitrarily as I once judged them." And, in response, he has "joined [his] countrymen in becoming more suspicious, more ingrown, more tribal, more cautious, more fearful." When the ghettoes swelter and he hears a siren in the distance, he wonders "if it is the final signal that cer-tain old white racist chickens are coming home to roost on my personal doorstep" (167). He rather suspects that is the case.

In the fall of 1971, only a few months after the publication of King's *Con-fessions,* appeared an even more compelling narrative of racial conversion,

Down to Now, by Pat Watters, veteran reporter of the Civil Rights Movement. The early 1970s, it seems, was a time to take stock: the movement was over and many of those who had participated in it or observed it at close hand were in a reflective mood. Watters had observed it at much closer hand than had King: he had covered the movement for the Atlanta *Journal* and then had written about race relations for the Southern Regional Council, that racially progressive body, based in Atlanta, of which James McBride Dabbs had been president. At first Watters had approached the movement as he had approached many other stories, as an interested but more-or-less dispassionate chronicler. But in 1961 and 1962, in a black church in south Georgia, that changed: Watters, a white Georgian of rather conventional racial leanings, was converted to the cause of racial justice. *Down to Now* is his story of that conversion, as well as of the Civil Rights Movement in its glory and its decline.

Two years before the publication of *Down to Now,* Watters had produced another book, *The South and the Nation* (1969), a more objective analysis of the problems and possibilities of Dixie. By the time he began *Down to Now* he had given himself over altogether to a more personal voice. Describing himself as "a white Southerner who did not participate in the movement—but whose life was essentially changed by it,"[16] he announces his intention to "convey, pay honor to, glorify, that life-giving spirit of the southern movement which did so much for the South and for countless people who felt it in their hearts—including myself" (ix). As he writes in 1970 and 1971 he tries to recapture what he had felt as he witnessed civil rights activity in Albany, Georgia, and other Deep South towns: "I have tried in my mind so many times, in so many ways to grasp the whole of this most elusive truth, finally beginning this writing to seek it from many different vantages . . . but not sure even yet if it is to be fully known, or even whether it is more than a fanciful projection merely of my own deeply personal reaction to the movement." What he saw and felt, he finally decides, was "extra-cultural, beyond the normal limits of American culture," and his own "inarticulateness . . . can be accounted for in terms of this extra-cultural quality" (10)—a quality that was nothing short of "the power of love" (11).

16. Pat Watters, *Down to Now: Reflections on the Civil Rights Movement* (New York, 1971), x. Hereafter cited in the text by page number.

Feeling he must tell his story for the reason all converts, religious or secular, have—simply the need to get it out, to connect with others—Watters
is compelled for another reason as well: "American culture is so desperately
in need of new alternatives" (11), and the love and brotherhood of the Civil
Rights Movement, if they could be recaptured, would provide a kind of
cultural salvation:

> If life in America were reasonably satisfactory for most of the inhabi-
> tants of the country, if the life of the world were not threatened by as-
> pects of American culture and its self-imposed limitations of direc-
> tions of change, then maybe I would not attach so much importance
> to what I think I saw and felt afoot in the southern movement. I
> would not be so anguished because what was there is seldom ex-
> pressed now, would not feel this compulsion to go back in memory
> and time and old, spent notebooks trying to find what was there in
> precise terms . . . trying, I guess, to find salvation. (11)

Salvation, "after all," Watters insists, "on the most forthright level, was
what the movement offered"—and what America missed (11).

It is clear, thus, that to Watters, as to Larry King, Sarah Patton Boyle,
and most of the other white racial converts, the Civil Rights Movement was
about much more than race. It was about personal and cultural salvation in
a broader sense. Part One of Watters's narrative is titled "A Southerner's
Quest: There Must Be a God Somewhere," and that title suggests the religious form his quest for racial salvation will take. His experience of racial
conversion begins, appropriately enough, in a church, a black church in Albany, Georgia, in the winter of 1961. Will Campbell has written that as a
child he had believed that all true southern religion lay in the white church,
that "Niggerchurch . . . had nothing to do with Christianity."[17] In fact,
Watters discovers, the Negro church had everything to do with Christianity, bringing together the Christian gospel and its application in society. As
he writes, he recalls the early civil rights meetings, which usually took place
in churches, recalls "the singing in the church, that incomparable music":
"The mass meetings and demonstrations that I saw in the early 1960s were
foremost for me a deep, personal awakening, in the real sense a religious ex-

17. Campbell, *Brother to a Dragonfly,* 108.

perience." He was "exalted" by what he saw and heard, "overwhelmed" by "the onrush and power of it" (3).

Watters recalls the thrill of his first experience, following the marchers out of the Shiloh Baptist Church onto the streets of Albany. He had walked into the church on a bleak and chilly day in December 1961 and had taken a seat on a back pew, so cold that he kept on his overcoat, and listened to the small band of worshipers and protesters, some in suits, some in work clothes, singing "the sweet and swelling, eloquent church [songs] of the movement" (4). Spellbound, he listened to a young black woman who earlier had been jailed for joining a group of Negroes gathered at the Albany city hall to pray "for the sins of the city fathers" (5). Holding a microphone in her white-gloved hands, "much as a priest [holds] the chalice," she leads her listeners out of the church, into the drizzling rain, toward the bus station cafeteria and their rendezvous with the white police and with jail. "They were just ordinary Negroes up there . . . south Georgia Negroes, their faces, postures the familiar ones of all the cooks and filling station attendants I had ever seen," but what they did was, to Watters, "incredible." As he followed the marchers out of the church, he was full of both a certain fear and, "despite it all, . . . an exhilaration, a sense unstoppable of joy" (6). He witnesses their arrest at the bus terminal lunchroom, for "protesting that they could not be served in this airless, dingy little place" (8) and marvels at what has occurred:

> I was seeing it for the first time and could not contain all the feeling and meaning of it, all that sense of fearsome forces that had hovered over all the consciousness of my growing up and living in the South, finally meeting, the brooding thunder heard far-off for a lifetime suddenly built to a full storm of lightning flashes, wild wind and a pelleting rain—all about me, all that irony, that bravery, that fear and that appalled or warily watching reaction of black and white Southerners looking on there at the bus terminal, as the arrests proceeded. (9)

This was Watters's awakening, a major phase of his racial conversion, described in the language—exhilaration, joy, thunder and lightning, the "onrush and power" of the moment—of religious conversions from the seventeenth-century Massachusetts Bay to the backwoods churches and tent revivals of twentieth-century Dixie. And it was but one of many such experiences for Watters, the reporter who had, despite himself, become spiritual participant. He recalls in particular the clear winter's night in 1961 when Martin Luther King, Jr., came to the Shiloh Baptist Church, "this time with every inch of it crowded, all the seats taken, people sitting and standing, filling the aisles and the vestibule," the singing "more fervent, more beautiful than I had yet heard it" (11). Watters, again witnessing an event "like nothing I had ever known" (12), listens as Ralph Abernathy exclaims, "I want the white man to be free" (13), then hears Martin Luther King, full of religious fervor, enrapture the crowd as a revivalist does his candidates for salvation. Looking back nearly a decade later, Watters reflects on that "miraculous night" (16) and on the Albany Movement of protests and demonstrations that followed. And he reflects too—for this is a parallel theme of his book—on the eventual decline of the spirit of the movement: "Somehow it got lost. Lost in Albany and lost in all the little Negro churches standing on the corners in all the cities and towns and country roads across the South where the movement entered into and was fed by the spirit of the Negro people" (19). "What happened?" Watters asks:

> Suddenly, once, white and Negro southern involvement in race came together in positiveness, creativeness, instead of the old destructiveness and, pushing beyond cultural limits to unknown exaltation, hope, mysticism, ecstacy, produced a shimmering vision of what life between the races might be, and more than that, what life in America for all people might be. Then it was gone. It took exactly ten years, the decade of the 1960s, for all of it, the rise and fall of it. (20)

After his intensely personal first chapter, Watters follows the pattern of all racial converts and digs into his own past to unearth those racial sins for which he must repent. He recalls his early education in Jim Crow: that one did not say Mr. and Mrs., sir and ma'am, to Negroes, but that one also did not, if one had the right upbringing, say "nigger." Watters realizes now, as he had not before, how black women sacrificed their own family lives to cook and wash for white families; but "few of us even thought about it. And how, *how* were we able to achieve such insensitivity, such cruelty, with never a pang of conscience?" (30). As a child growing up in Georgia—even living for a time in Albany—Watters was aware of lynchings and other racial atrocities, but even more than that, he realizes, "it was the everyday cruelty, the ongoing grinding down of people, the hopelessness more than the physical helplessness, the petty and banal cruelty and the terrible economic disadvantage, which should have been apparent to even the most blind, most bigoted of us." "How blind we had been made to be," he repeats. The South had been an "evil system" (34), and by his consent he had been a part of that evil.

One finds echoes of Lillian Smith in much of what Watters says. As a child, he is taken into the black section of town by the woman who cares for him, and he senses there a vast ease and friendliness; he "perhaps . . . perceived a superior sense of community, and perhaps for the first time, so early, began to know that all was not perfect in my parents' world." "It was comfortable, familiar, being with Negroes," he had discovered. "Communication was easier." Nor was there the anxiety about "that nether-world of cuss words and sex that in the lingering Victorianism of the South of my growing up came quite early in life to fascinate us, frighten us, torment our consciences" (27–28). Like Smith, Watters recalls the conspiracy of silence of his childhood South, both blacks and whites "never conceding, never speaking," beneath the surface of harmonious race relations, "the secret knowledge . . . of evil in the situation, evil brooding over us, ever treacherously threatening that giddy and gay talk which, by its sheer will, kept the wretched, patched-up thing alive" (31). And, like Smith, Watters decries a racial system that added to what was, in the best of cases, "the loneliness of existence": "The persistent, pathetic effort to reach others with love is man's most magnificent impulse; the imposition of such a system as that which used to be, in the South, deliberately setting up barriers to this already most difficult of all things to do, is surely insane, surely the worst sin" (38).

Watters speaks less of the specific racial sins of the fathers than others in the conversion genre, but it is clear that he is still "blind" as he enters young manhood. As a reporter for the Atlanta *Journal* in the early 1950s he viewed race politically, not morally. He sensed that "the big story, the one transcending all others," was to be race, yet "I had no awareness at all of the background of struggle for Negro rights" (45). Thus he "missed the meaning" of the Montgomery bus boycott of 1955–56, "was oblivious to the subsequent Prayer Pilgrimage to Washington in May 1957 . . . and to a

Youth March Dr. King led in 1959 with 40,000 in attendance" (50). Not until the summer of 1960, when he was sent to the Atlanta airport to meet a plane carrying King (whom he had never before even seen), returning from jail after having been arrested in a sit-in, did Watters sense the impulse and the power of the Civil Rights Movement. Not until then did he sense that the movement was not only for southern blacks but was also for himself. Following King's car to the Ebenezer Baptist Church in downtown Atlanta, Watters sees the car stop at the DeKalb-Fulton county line, hailed by a group of black students and sit-in veterans who have come to greet King. Listening to the students sing "We Shall Overcome"—"I had not heard the song before, did not catch all the words"—he nonetheless felt "all through me the spirit of it, its force and its meaning" (54), was profoundly moved in a manner he had not expected.

The spirit Watters sensed was that same spirit Lillian Smith, James McBride Dabbs, Sarah Patton Boyle, and Will Campbell had sensed before him, but the language, the cadences, Watters fell back on to express himself were more nearly William Faulkner's:

> I stood on the shoulder of the road, listening, and out of a lifetime of the way it used to be, out of knowledge of love forbidden, the hovering, hidden, unspoken knowledge of evil and wrong, out of all my life of acquiesence in the evil and *their* acquiesence, Negro acquiesence, our mutual acquiesence making the evil seem immutable and the South hopeless, and, most of all, out of all I knew of the striving of Negro and white Southerners to reach each other, love each other through barriers of evil, the potential for good in such strivings—out of all my southern experience, I listened and heard them saying in the song that the way things used to be was no more, was forever ended. And knowing all that that meant for them, and for me, I cried. I cried for the first time in many years, cried unabashedly, cried for joy—and hope. (54)

Watters's conversion on the road to Fulton County—more than a year before his experience in the Albany church—he describes as something completely unanticipated, but, more than he knew, he must have been ready to be converted. Such—the *conviction* of one's sinfulness—always preceded the conversion itself.

In any case, after "We Shall Overcome" and its message "entered, invaded" his life, Watters was not tempted to backslide. As one of the newly converted, he found himself "increasingly impatient" with those who had not seen the light, "intolerant of all those who had not harkened to it, moderate friends spouting fashionable cant, racist neighbors." People he had "tolerated, enjoyed in one way or another," became offensive (55). The racist politicians, often charming and amusing, whom he had earlier humored, he now could not tolerate: "after having seen a few towns in the grip of their cynicism delivering cruel blows to the great morality of the movement, I lost my taste for them, could never again stand around with them talking their language of tricks and evasiveness and laughing with them their cynical laughter at the rest of the world out there." The spirituality and the power of the Civil Rights Movement not only made "the commonplace rituals of the society I lived in, the white society, seem pale by contrast" but also "spoke a condemnation that made them, too, unpalatable." When in a group Watters heard "The Star-Spangled Banner" and looked around and saw no African Americans, he felt like singing no more. When he observed a Boy Scout awards banquet and saw no black faces, he found it difficult to accept the three-fingered salute and singing and "hollering sentimentality" (56). The early 1960s brought "a process of alienation for me, alienation from the South and the society I was raised in and thought I knew," and the alienation from white society "drove me more and more often to the movement, deeper and deeper into its meaning," into its "joy and hopefulness" (57).

More than any other of the racial converts, save perhaps Patty Boyle, Watters seems to be emotionally moved by what he sees and hears. His tone is often zealous, his language sometimes excessive, as the tone and language of the freshly redeemed tend to be. From his vantage point of 1970, he listens to tapes of the earlier mass meetings and, particularly, their music and, with tears in his eyes, feels "the old, choked aching joy and, for a second, the old leap of hope, boundless hope" (57). He recalls all the times he heard demonstrators sing "We Shall Overcome"—in the Albany Movement of 1961–62, the Birmingham campaign of 1963 and 1964, the campaigns in St. Augustine in 1964 and Selma in 1965, in voter registration meetings across the South, and at the mourning for Medgar Evers in Mississippi and for the black Birmingham schoolgirls, victims of the Sixteenth Street Bap-

tist Church bombing in 1963. As the early fervor of the Civil Rights Movement waned and cynicism set in, he heard it sung listlessly in 1967 and
1968. And he heard it sung, finally, at the funeral of Martin Luther King in
Atlanta in April 1968—"but who, even in the instant's lift of the music in
the heart, could at such a time believe?" (62). Watters himself had sung the
song the night news came of King's death, seated with nine or ten other
mourners, joining hands with them, "as once it had been done in the
churches," singing "in all our grief and despair and hopelessness." Watters
depicts himself as one of the deeply stricken, one who had gone from hopelessness to the spirit of "hope and joy" of the movement, "only to be
plunged at the decade's end" by King's death into "a hopelessness beyond
hopelessness, like a man who has tasted for a little time true happiness and
then lost it" (62).

Watters concludes his long first section with the death of King, but then
goes back—for a brief period, more the historian than the participant—to
trace those early years of the movement that he had missed altogether. A
sort of latter-day Quentin Compson, discovering facts but fearing he is
missing part of the truth, he worries that he is "romanticizing, imposing my
own southern bias and wistful, desperate hoping on such things as these
memories of the reality of the sit-ins and freedom rides. . . . I keep asking
people who were there if I am wrong . . . in thinking the theme of redemptive love was so much a part of those early events. They assure me that I am
not" (109). He feels more comfortable when he again considers Albany, the
next great campaign after the freedom rides and the point in the movement
at which his own involvement had begun.

In his mind he returns once more to Albany's Shiloh Baptist Church,
not in the chill of winter this time but in the heat of a south Georgia summer, nightly finding himself sitting on the floor beneath the pulpit. As the
people in the sanctuary behind him sing the "unaccompanied, hand-
clapping music of the movement" (142), he feels the songs carrying him to
a "mysterious, unknown place" (145) and gives himself "to the sweat and
the heat and the music, a sense almost of loss of self, of having blended into
all the other sweating bodies . . . and the great feeling alive in the church"
(142). Watters, the reporter, has gone to take notes, but he finds himself
neglecting his professional duties. He does report briefly on the emerging
struggle between King's Southern Christian Leadership Conference and the

more militant SNCC, but there always exists in his mind "the powerful pounding of the music of the mass meetings as a counterpoint to my words of discovery and analysis" (150). Watters repeats the phrases "give myself" and "gave myself"—to the music, to the spirit of the movement—and as he does throughout the book when he is most emotionally moved, he resorts to rhetorical excess, a sort of Faulknerian stream of consciousness:

> And memories, images building within me the awareness—not understanding or full comprehension, just the simple awareness of something entirely new, a spirit suddenly alive in dead America (and my own career-concentrated, deadened sensibilities), full of heady portent, a snapping loose suddenly of bonds in a process that, once begun, could not be stopped until all were gone, not just some of them, but all, so that those of us who had been by history and conditioning completely tied down were to be completely free—whether we wanted to be, could without fear, or not.

"It is so hard now to recapture the feeling of that great time," writes Watters nearly a decade later (160–61).

In the pages that follow, Watters alternates between his role as reporter and his newly found identity as convert. Back in Atlanta, after his first stay in Albany in December 1961, he had reflected on his experiences: "It was as though I had been in some mystical new land, had seen and sensed the surface of its miracles and promise, and then, as in a dream, was gone from it." But when he returned to the Shiloh Baptist Church six months later, "it was as though nothing had changed, nothing had happened, as though no time had passed and, as in a dream, that which had so stirred me and changed my life in December had been held frozen in the intervening months and now with magic, in a moment, had returned to life" (171). Again, the freedom songs move him most. Even in 1970, hearing them on tape, he returns to "the mystical, inspired and excited, ecstatic—and reverent mood of those meetings" (180).

Mixed with the exaltation of Watters's Albany experience was sheer terror. Indeed, the "unreasoning fear . . . of southern white racism" (145)—and, even more, the "fear of fear" itself (224)—had been the "foremost motivation" for his going to Albany in the first place: "All my life I had been afraid—full of large fears, small fears, all the accumulation of fears that are in part normal. . . fears . . . never fully known, fully faced, understood" (227). In fact, his fear of the extremes of southern racism was not "unreasoning" at all: in his childhood hometown of Albany his motel phone was tapped, his tires were slashed, sugar was poured into his gas tank, and he was trailed on the highway as he drove back to Albany after attending a meeting in a still remoter part of rural south Georgia. Later he experienced even greater fear when the movement took him into Alabama and Mississippi, where "we lived with the knowledge that there was often virtually no distinction between police and the worst terrorist elements, including the Klan." He overcame his fear at such times, Watters writes, by focusing on the music, the spirit, of the movement, "the love I had come to feel . . . the mystical, ecstatic experience I found in the mass meetings" (226): "Suddenly I knew that I felt more alive, more complete, more happy than I ever had before in my life" (227).

The feeling could not last. In the fourth section of his narrative, titled "The Fall," Watters laments the decline of the early spirit of Albany, the spirit that found its most eloquent expression in Martin Luther King's "I Have a Dream" speech in Washington in August 1963. The following month, in Birmingham, he stands in the midst of the shattered stained-glass windows and scattered Sunday School lessons, and realizes that it was in just such sanctuaries of black churches throughout the South that he himself had found a kind of salvation. Such churches had become to him "the only places where I had ever experienced real religious feeling, in a lifetime within the South's church-oriented society, growing up in the Methodist Episcopal Church South." He stands and stares, "unable to cry or even be angry, only numbly sorrowful—for the church, the people, the movement, what had been done to religion there, but most of all, in a sickened sense of defeat, sorrowful for the South" (272).

Even after Birmingham—in some measure, especially after Birmingham—Watters seeks refuge in the black church. Covering the movement in St. Augustine in 1964, he finds himself sitting beneath the altar on the floor of a church, listening to the demonstrators sing "Amazing Grace" and reflecting on the "meaning and truth and simple hope of the movement": "It was still so good to return to such moments from ugliness and harshness and immerse myself, sitting in the hot church, sweating, losing some of myself in the meeting" (288). And as he followed the marchers in St. Augustine, aware of "the terrible danger, the uncontrolled mob awaiting" them, he nonetheless felt—still feels as he writes—"the exhilaration, the joy that welled up in me . . . I threw back my head in exultation. This is the place to be, I said; this is where I belong" (7). In the terror of covering, that same year, Mississippi Freedom Summer, in despair over the split between SNCC and the SCLC, the "imposition of all kinds of ideologies on the essentially simple, religion-based, civil libertarian idealism of the southern movement" (306), he still returns to the memories of Albany: "I heard their songs and saw their faces, and once again . . . I found myself crying—not this time just out of hope still inherent in such a thing as had happened in Albany, not now just out of the joy of knowing old evil was dying, but now simply and unabashedly out of love, love of a great people, good people" (371).

Watters concludes his narrative by attempting to make sense of the Civil Rights Movement and his own emotional involvement in it. He describes the "mood of hopelessness" he endured after Martin Luther King, Jr.'s death and "the sad finale to [King's] efforts" (382), the Poor People's Campaign of 1968. Like Larry King and other white racial converts, Watters mourns the death of the spirit of the early movement, that spirit in which African Americans seemed to give whites a second chance, the period, he believes, before SNCC and its "northern influence" came finally "to see whites and American society as totally evil . . . upsetting the balance of love and hate" (403). As he writes in 1971, he realizes that he has "been seeking since the [James] Meredith March and Dr. King's death some kind of philosophical adjustment to all that the years of the movement meant to me" (381).

In the end the same question might be asked concerning Watters that I asked about Sarah Patton Boyle. Did he expect too much of the movement? Did he truly understand what it was about? Did he expect the movement to do too much for *himself*? Watters does not avoid such questions altogether. "Was it ever there at all?" he wonders, "what I believed I saw and felt in the little churches of the movement? Sometimes, sometimes, I suspect myself of having all unconsciously shaped my thought about the southern movement on that most southern, most misleading model—harking back to a golden age and lamenting all the disruption and disintegration that has come upon us" (381). On one occasion, as he attends a rally in the late 1960s and catches himself thinking that the music is no longer so moving as it once was, he accuses himself of a certain self-indulgence: "I felt foolish . . . sitting there concerned over so frivolous a thing as the spiritual quality of the music when children were starving and human dignity was still being destroyed in the black belt" (392). Even earlier, when he had been most emotionally involved in the movement, as he had followed the marchers in St. Augustine and had experienced a feeling of "exultation," he had also for a moment "felt bad" for "somehow exploiting this great and serious thing that the Negroes were doing, and their suffering" (7).

But writing in 1970 and 1971, Watters defends his exultation and his involvement: "instead of the shame I think a lot of whites used to feel about their undeniable joy in the mighty doings of the movement, we should have felt proud. For we came as close as whites have in America to responding appropriately to the movement" (7). He recognizes that the movement filled for him and for others a "religious" need—it was "not unlike the best ecstatic experience in the fundamentalist churches of the white South" (412)—but he also believes that the spirit of the Civil Rights Movement, if heeded, could redeem a region and a nation as well as an individual. That spirit "set out to heal the insanity in southern society, to end the sin of it, to allow expiation of it" (38). And its impact transcended the South:

> In broadest terms, I think what happened was that the movement, which started out seeking to overthrow the southern segregationist order, eventually challenged all that at the core of American culture which could have allowed such an order, as one symptom of a system-wide sickness, to exist for a century under the American Constitution. (379–80)

But in the final analysis Watters's relation to the Civil Rights Movement must be read in intensely personal terms. In the latter days of the movement, the late sixties, when he and others had nearly given up on it, he attends a civil rights gathering in west Tennessee, and, for the first time in nearly a decade of covering the movement, he is called upon to speak. Unprepared for the moment, he stumbles and stammers, but given a second chance, a couple of nights later, he rises as a representative of "the city . . . where people seem all discouraged, seem to have given up on America," expresses gratitude to the applauding black audience for its "hopefulness," its will and determination, and experiences a moment of that "exaltation" he had seen in other speakers during the heyday of the movement (400). His was an expression of gratitude for all the Civil Rights Movement had done for him—for the manner in which it had lifted him out of the "commonplace," had "freed" him. It was also a tribute—as indeed, in a longer form, *Down to Now* was to be—to a time, in the early and mid-1960s, when some few people, mostly black but sometimes white, seemed better than he had thought people could be, more patient, forgiving, sacrificing, and loving, producing as dramatic a demonstration of practical Christianity as the nation had ever seen. If that spirit could not last, that was just because human nature would not allow it: African Americans could not turn the other cheek forever.

IV

CURIOUS INTERSECTIONS

Race and Class at Century's End

BY THE 1980s the racial conversion narrative had fully arrived, had in fact become such a frequent form of expression that books of that description had come to constitute a fully realized, if little acknowledged, southern literary subgenre. The words "Confession" and "Conversion" used in a secular context (usually but not always referring specifically to race) had become staples in titles of southern memoirs: one thinks not only of Larry King's *Confessions of a White Racist* but also Florence King's amusing and insightful *Confessions of a Failed Southern Lady* (1985) as well as *The Conversion of a Klansman* (1979), by Thomas Tarrants—a born-again Alabamian "overcome with a sense of [his] sinfulness, . . . hideous and wretched," "blind all [his] life" until, in prison, he "received [his] sight"[1]—and, of course, Styron's fictional *Confessions of Nat Turner* (1967), which was in certain respects, as I have suggested, the Confessions of William Styron. Still to come was *The Confession of Dorothy Danner* (1995), the story of a white racial rebel who falls short of full repentance, as well as numerous other memoirs that could well have borne the title "Confession" or "Conversion."

The memoirs proliferated even as a new mythology, seemingly at odds with the old racial benightedness, came to be associated with Dixie—not, after 1980, the old mythology grounded in the realities of southern defeat, poverty, failure, and general backwardness but rather the mythology of the

---

1. Thomas A. Tarrants, III, *The Conversion of a Klansman* (Garden City, N.Y., 1979), x, viii.

Sun Belt with its vision of gleaming new cities, resort "properties," Olympian successes, political victories (two presidents in two decades), and general prosperity and optimism—a South, that is, no longer so noticeably haunted by God and not seeming to take sin and guilt *or* redemption so seriously as it earlier had. No matter. Even the triumph of Peachtree Street, the magic of southern public relations in the newest of New Souths, could not prevent white southerners from pouring out memoirs about growing up racially sinful in Dixie. In 1983, without being very specific, I wrote of this phenomenon: "The confessional literature has already become in part, one suspects, a habit in the South, a function, an aesthetic ritual. The creative Southerner who leaves his home now writes the obligatory confessional because his predecesors have." In those same random remarks I also wondered if, despite the continuing stream of works of southern self-exploration, the new southern confessional literature would demonstrate the same urgency and intensity as the old writing, if it would be written from "the same mixture of love and anger, shame and pride" that had driven the works of such charter members of the southern school of shame and guilt as W. J. Cash and Lillian Smith—if, that is, "an all-consuming passion to explain" would "constitute the basis for future Southern writing."[2]

I still wonder that to some degree—wonder, that is, whether the contemporary white southern memoirist or social commentator can feel quite the same intensity in writing about race, the same anguish and tension in his or her telling, now that telling the racial truth about the South and about oneself means not (as it did for Cash and Smith, not to mention such earlier truth-telling southerners as George W. Cable) risk to property and reputation and physical and emotional well-being but rather a few kind remarks on southern book pages. I certainly understand the *impulse* to write about an earlier benighted South and about one's participation in its barbarities: there is, after all, something about tortured old Dixie that is so much more compelling, more exciting, than anything in the sanitized New South—and confession, after all, is good for the soul. The situation, in one respect, is not so very much different from that of young southerners of artistic bent in the 1920s and 1930s who, before they moved into a new age,

---

2. Fred Hobson, *Tell About the South: The Southern Rage to Explain* (1983; reprint, Baton Rouge, 1998), 15–16.

took a backward glance (to borrow Allen Tate's phrase) at what they had left behind. And thus certain of today's white southerners of heightened racial sensitivity and literary bent who came of age in the 1940s, 1950s, or 1960s take their own backward glances, this time not at the Good Old Days but rather at the Bad Old Days, when the southern drama was so much more exciting, before they become full citizens of the South Triumphant.

Much of this, of course, is highly speculative. What is certain, however, is that the South has indeed seen, since the mid-1980s, an even greater outpouring of narratives of white racial awakening than in any previous ten- or fifteen-year period. I count a dozen or more works that would fall into that category, many of them by younger southerners, but I should like to discuss first a relatively recent narrative by a member of the old guard—nearly of the generation of Smith and Lumpkin—who did, for a time, pay a price for her apostasy. Virginia Durr's autobiography, *Outside the Magic Circle,* is often rambling and unguarded—qualities, in fact, that contribute to its honesty and its power. If her story, narrated when she was in her seventies, sometimes seems hardly to qualify as conversion narrative at all, it is only because its author does not confess to having been so great a sinner in the first place as some of her contemporaries: even as a child, she insists, she detested segregation and racial discrimination, and thus there would seem to be little racism for her to come up from. But if she does not need to repent for herself, she certainly needs to repent for the sins of her Alabama fathers, who, at best, were racial paternalists. She had grown up admiring the Reconstruction-era Ku Klux Klan, to which her grandfather had belonged, as "something noble and grand and patriotic that had saved the white women of the South."[3]

At times in her memoir, then, Durr proves herself more a product of a racist system than she earlier suggests. Like Sarah Patton Boyle, the daughter of a minister and herself one generation removed from the slaveholding planter class, Durr grows up surrounded by black servants, finding herself particularly attached to her nurse, who was "as much a symbol of safety to

---

3. Virginia Durr, *Outside the Magic Circle: The Autobiography of Virginia Foster Durr,* ed. Hollinger F. Barnard (Tuscaloosa, 1985), 44. Hereafter cited in the text by page number.

me as my mother was" (14). She had admired as well another black woman, an old ex-slave, whose intelligence made it difficult for young Virginia Foster "to swallow the prevailing theory that blacks were inferior" (5). But when she leaves the South for college at Wellesley, she has the same awakening that James McBride Dabbs and Katharine Lumpkin had at Columbia. When Durr finds a young African American woman sitting at her table in the dormitory dining room, all her notions of racial equality flee:

> I nearly fell over dead. . . . I promptly got up, marched out of the room, went upstairs, and waited for the head of the house to come. . . . I told her that I couldn't possibly eat at the table with a Negro girl. I was from Alabama and my father would have a fit . . . he would die. . . . She would have to move me immediately. (56)

After the head of house refuses to move Virginia and, further, tells her that she will have to leave school if she does not conform to the rules of the house, Durr—in the tradition of racial converts from Huck Finn forward—has a decision to make: "I stayed awake all night long. It was terrible for me, because I knew if my father ever heard of it, he would be furious. . . . I had been taught that if I ate at the table with a Negro girl I would be committing a terrible sin against society" (57–58). Durr decides to eat with the African American girl, but hardly for the noblest of reasons: she likes Wellesley and hates the thought of leaving. At first she feels a certain shame in breaking the southern taboo. But the incident at Wellesley turned out to be "the origin of a doubt" (59).

Later Durr comes to realize that "it wasn't the Negro girl I was afraid of. It was my father's reaction I feared" (58). It is one of several times in the narrative that she—like Smith and Lumpkin before her—reports an incident that reflects badly on the father she presumes to admire and cherish. The Reverend Dr. Foster, schooled in Presbyterian rectitude at Princeton and Edinburgh, is depicted at first as an honorable and enlightened man— and one so courageous that he is dismissed from his pulpit in Birmingham because he will not give in to his parishioners' demand that he preach the literal truth of the Bible. But as Durr's narrative continues, she paints, whether altogether consciously or not, a less attractive picture of her father. He emerges as a rather weak man, spoiled by his wife, daughters, and servants, able to do little for himself. Unable to make a steady living after his dismissal from his church, he brings Virginia home from Wellesley after her second year—not because of her association with African Americans but rather because he cannot afford the expense and has too much pride to let her live in the self-help house, where she could have paid her own way. In racial matters as well, Sterling Foster emerges as something other than the enlightened paternalist Durr had earlier described. A registrar in Birmingham, he takes pride in disqualifying every potential African American voter who comes before him, boasting on one occasion that he found a way to turn down "a damn nigger . . . who had been to Harvard." Durr accepted his action because "Daddy was just upholding pure white Southern womanhood and white supremacy" (102).

Is Durr being as sarcastic as she sounds? More likely, she is simply reflecting her honest reaction at the time. But, in a more general sense, does she fully realize all she is saying about her father? After all, she is in her seventies as she tells her story, and since she is dictating, rather than writing, her memoir, she perhaps takes less care than she otherwise might have. The word "patriarchy" never appears in Durr's narrative, but it is clear to the reader, if perhaps not to Durr, that she closely identifies her father (as well as her Klansman grandfather) with the old, corrupt southern system, with white supremacy and segregation—and in rejecting the one she is in some measure rejecting the other. Indeed, Durr went on to reject Dixie's racial status quo as fully as any other white southerner of her generation save perhaps Lillian Smith, finding segregation altogether unacceptable as early as the 1930s—when she lived in Washington with her husband, Clifford Durr, an official in the Roosevelt administration. Later she would become vice-chairman of the National Committee to Abolish the Poll Tax—thus, whether consciously or not, challenging her registrar father's notions about African American voters. After moving back to Alabama in 1951, she would take a strong stand in support of the Civil Rights Movement, making her Montgomery home the primary outpost of white racial liberalism in Alabama. It was the Depression, Durr later said, that had fully awakened her, had shocked her out of "being well-born": "I saw a blinding light like Saul on the road to Damascus" (xi). Not only was she awakened to racial discrimination but also to poverty and economic injustice in a larger sense. Her battles from that point on, however, would be fought largely on the southern racial front.

One comes away from Durr's narrative with a conviction that her conversion to racial justice was a deep and lasting one. It had also come about for reasons more various and complicated than might at first appear—largely, indeed, because of her belief that segregation was morally wrong, but also because she believed that it was, quite simply, bad manners: "I was brought up to be a Southern lady, and it dawned on me how rude it was to think a black was too dirty and smelled too bad to sit by me" (121–22). If in her adherence to manners she still belonged to the world of her fathers and mothers (although applying their code of manners in a fashion altogether unacceptable to them), she also held to that earlier world in other ways. A racial paternalist, in some measure, she remained to the end, living in Alabama, sounding very much like William Alexander Percy of Mississippi, complaining of the white man's burden: "It's a wonder we were able to stay as sane as we did—or as solvent. . . . A lot of Negroes . . . depended on the Durr family as they had for years and years. They looked to us to get them out of jail or to get them in the hospital or lend them money" (324). And she also remained, just as staunchly as Patty Boyle, a firm believer in breeding. Indeed, the most disparaging adjective in her arsenal is "common": George Wallace supporters were "common-as-pig-tracks people" (314), and so were a number of other poor white southerners for whom Virginia Durr had no use. Her education in poverty during the Great Depression—her awakening to life on "the other side of the tracks"—went only so far. Still she viewed with utter disgust "the poor white trash":

> They were totally uncouth, very miserable people with either tobacco or snuff dripping down their chins. They were always yellow; somehow, I think it must have been malaria. And they had pellegra and hookworms and they bred "like rabbits." They were completely beyond the pale. (46)

Racism Durr conquered as well as any other white southerner of her generation, but never was she able to come up fully from classism.

To expect Virginia Durr to do otherwise is perhaps to expect too much. Her story, in any case, is one of the most compelling of those traditional racial narratives to appear in the past decade and a half. Other recent memoirs—I think of Reynolds Price's *Clear Pictures* (1989) and Elizabeth Spencer's *Landscapes of the Heart* (1998)—do not seem in the beginning to be particularly about race, but both, as they develop, turn into personal racial histories. Other autobiographical works, such as Lewis Killian's *Black and White* (1994), focus completely on race. A Georgia-born sociologist, a self-described "Cracker" who had pondered race relations for more than a half-century, Killian tells the story of his "conversion from southern ortho-doxy," recalling in particular a moment of racial awakening in his early twenties which he describes as a "cleansing experience": "I had been bap-tized in the waters of a river I had never entered before, and the first layer of years' accumulation of feelings of white supremacy had been washed away."[4] Still other recent works—Ellen Douglas's *Truth: Four Stories I Am Finally Old Enough to Tell* and Edward Ball's *Slaves in the Family,* both pub-lished in 1998—are attempts to come to terms with family guilt more than with personal guilt.

Douglas, Spencer, and Price, of course, have all dealt with race in their fiction, but none has dealt with it so personally and so directly as in their re-cent memoirs. Douglas undertakes *Truth*—or, rather, her lengthy essay "On Second Creek," which makes up nearly half the book—after she comes upon historian Winthrop Jordan's study, *Tumult and Silence at Sec-ond Creek* (1993), which tells the story of an alleged plot of a slave uprising in Adams County, Mississippi, in May 1861—and the execution, by order of a committee of "the gentlemen of the neighborhood," that September and October of some thirty slaves who may or may not have been guilty of insurrection. Douglas reads Jordan's book with particular interest because her own family had owned a farm on Second Creek for nearly two hundred years and her own ancestors had played some part in the 1861 proceedings. Just what part Douglas seeks to discover as she visits the archives of Louisi-ana State University, where four pages of notes on the incident, taken down in 1861, are kept, and then interviews a number of people, white and black, who she hopes will help her to arrive at the truth. When she first reads of the incident, she is astounded not only that it had occurred but that "such a huge event in the history of a small county [was not] known to me." In her immediate family, lynching had been "unspeakable." And her "ances-tors, the portraits on the walls—they had been kind masters who treated

---

4. Lewis M. Killian, *Black and White: Reflections of a White Southern Sociologist* (Dix Hill, N.Y., 1994), 20, 26, 29.

their slaves with consistent humanity."[5] Or had they? She never finds out
for sure, nor ever uncovers the extent of her ancestors' culpability at Second
Creek.

Edward Ball's search for the truth about his family's racial sins is a more
extensive one, taking him all around the United States and, finally, to Sierra
Leone—where he faces his "responsibility" and participates in a "ceremony
of commemoration" on the banks of a creek from which captured slaves
were sent to the West African coast to be taken by white traders to America.
If the sins of the fathers are indeed visited upon succeeding generations,
Ball has a lot to answer for: he is the descendant of one of the South's
largest slaveholding families. Between 1698 and 1865, he estimates, "close
to four thousand black people were born into slavery to the Balls or bought
by them." Growing up primarily in South Carolina, the son of an Episcopal priest (the family seat was near Charleston), but attending college in
New England and settling in New York City, Ball at first was not particularly concerned with his family's racial past. That concern began when he
attended a large family reunion in the Carolina low country, after which he
determined to look into family history—a task made easier by Ball family
archives in North and South Carolina, as well as the willingness of the descendants of Ball family slaves to talk with him. He makes the discoveries
one might expect—that, despite family claims that Ball slaves had always
been treated "very well," such had not always been the case; that the family
had been involved not only in slavery but also, at least through marriage, in
the largest slave-trading operation in the British colonies; and that (a discovery, it seems, of every prober into family racial secrets from Isaac Mc-
Caslin on) the Ball patriarchs had also had children by their slaves and had
thus begun parallel black family lines. Ball insists several times that he feels
no personal "guilt" for the actions of his ancestors; rather he asserts, also
more than once, that he feels "accountability" for their sins and feels
"called upon to explain" their actions: the "slave business" was a "crime
that has not fully been acknowledged," and he must acknowledge that
crime. Of several descendants of Ball slaves he asks "forgiveness"; on one
occasion, when he brings an old black woman back to the delapidated

5. Ellen Douglas, *Truth: Four Stories I Am Finally Old Enough to Tell* (Chapel Hill,
1998), 192, 196.

cabin in which she had been born ninety years earlier, he weeps; and at the end, on the banks of the creek in Sierra Leone, he seeks expiation.[6] But except for these incidents (and unlike many of the earlier racial converts), Ball is relatively unemotional as he goes about his task of discovering the truth and accepting family "accountability." The reason, of course, is that the sins he recounts are not his own. For this reason, *Slaves in the Family* is, in tone, a curiously impersonal book.

Such is hardly the case with the memoirs of Price and Spencer, southerners a generation older than Ball who came of age in a harshly segregated South and for a time, by their inaction, seemed to give their tacit approval to that South. Price's early racial history is similar to those histories of Willie Morris, Pat Watters, and others who grew up middle class, small town, and content—in Price's case, in eastern North Carolina, the son of parents who were "at constant pains to be civil to every black they met, and . . . chided me fiercely when I once said *nigger*," but who nonetheless "held to the racial assumptions of their culture." Looking back from the vantage of the late 1980s, Price speaks of his family's—and his own—"willing involvement . . . in a blind and slow-paced evil," of the "evil world" he had inhabited. Price's racial "conversion"—he uses the term more than once—he attributes to his growing respect for the family yardman and his father's friend, Grant Terry, and, most of all, his introduction, in a Raleigh auditorium when he was thirteen or fourteen, to the great African American contralto Marian Anderson, an encounter that "changed [his] life":

> If I'd absorbed any of the racial convictions of my world—and how could I not?—I was changed down deep, in that one night. A woman had done it and mostly without words. I couldn't speak German, Italian or French; but I understood the spirituals. . . . In those two hours Marian Anderson led me through an immeasurably complex equation to an answer as simple and irrefutable as sunlight—God endowed this dark woman with this immense gift, the grandest I'd faced; the racial laws of the place I lived in, the people I loved, were wrong and evil. I would not obey and would find ways to change them.

That Price, "after my [1947] conversion in her presence," did not do more to change them, he later regrets. Although he rationalizes, when the

---

6. Edward Ball, *Slaves in the Family* (New York, 1998), 442–43, 7, 14, 416.

Civil Rights Movement bursts forth, that he would be less effective as a marcher and protester than as a "resident exile . . . silen[t] and cunning," moving "with watchful freedom through the heart of the enemy," he later realizes that he "might have found ways to be more actively involved in the heat of the struggle": "Now when I see films of the flocking brave faces, black and white, of the early rights movement . . . I'm more than sorry that my face is missing." "All these years late," he finds, "my silence offends me."[7]

Elizabeth Spencer's moment of full racial awakening, though more dramatic and involving greater personal sacrifice, came later in her life than Price's—as perhaps befits one born, in Mississippi, a decade earlier. Spencer had grown up the privileged and precocious daughter of the Deep South gentry; in fact, in the first three-quarters of her memoir she has little to say about racial conflict. She does acknowledge her family's gentle paternalism and expresses her own early fondness for blacks and her belief that they sometimes received a raw deal. But her involvement did not become personal until, in her thirties and a published novelist, she returned to Mississippi from Rome, where she had spent the previous two years as a Guggenheim fellow. She arrived home in September 1955, just after—"not many miles over in the Delta, and quite near my father's farm"—Emmett Till, a black teenager visiting from Chicago, had been beaten to death and thrown into the Sunflower River. His crime was apparently whistling at a white woman. Believing that her father—whose racial beliefs she had considered enlightened—would agree with her, Spencer spoke up, deploring the murder of Emmett Till. But her father "refused to discuss it or to hear any discussion of it. He said that 'we had to keep things in hand.' " Breaking with her father, her ears "ringing with parental abuse," Spencer left immediately for Oxford, Mississippi, and then for New York, knowing "in my bones, in the sick empty feeling there inside . . . *You don't belong down here anymore.*" To New York she would take the manuscript of her novel, *The Voice at the Back Door*—a cry for racial justice in Mississippi that would be published, to great acclaim, the following year. "I did not write the book to reform anybody except myself," Spencer explains:

7. Reynolds Price, *Clear Pictures* (New York, 1989), 85, 119, 259, 110–12, 118, 76, 261.

For I also had subscribed to the "Southern way of life," had thought that my parents and grandparents could not be wrongheaded. . . . But an accumulation of experience . . . had gradually begun to pile up on the scales and outweigh my received ideas. I wrote to straighten myself out, letting my story and the characters in it lead me on.[8]

The memoirs of Spencer and Price, published by major New York houses, have deservedly received a great deal of attention. Receiving far less notice, but in some cases equally revealing, are several works, written primarily by younger southerners, published by southern university presses in the late 1980s and early 1990s. Indeed, the proliferation of southern racial memoirs in the past decade has been aided by the decision of many university presses to publish what has come to be known as creative nonfiction—which, with southern presses, has often meant growing-up-southern memoirs, some of them better than others, and most of them more or less narratives of racial conversion. I say more or less; in fact, many of the memoirists do not seem to have been, compared with most of their predecessors, such intense racial sinners in the first place but were rather what the Puritans might have called half-way sinners who found themselves in the midst of a racially sinful society. I have in mind such memoirs as Melton McLaurin's *Separate Pasts: Growing Up White in the Segregated South* (1987), Melany Neilson's *Even Mississippi* (1989), Gayle Graham Yates's *Mississippi Mind: A Personal Cultural History* (1990), and Margaret Jones Bolsterli's *Born in the Delta: Reflections on the Making of a Southern White Sensibility* (1991).

These narratives share a number of qualities. Each of the authors grew up in the rural South at or just after midcentury, and all believed they knew African Americans intimately—but later realized they did not. Each, especially McLaurin, speaks of racial guilt. Each confesses early racial sins: McLaurin's abuse, in his North Carolina town, of a black man who had befriended him; Bolsterli's refusal to intervene when a black man, who was carrying her bag, is thrown out of her train car; Yates's and Neilson's uncritical acceptance of their families' and society's view that, in Neilson's words, "blacks were lesser human beings." Each of the authors experiences a racial awakening: Bolsterli as a high-school student in the Arkansas Delta, when a

8. Elizabeth Spencer, *Landscapes of the Heart* (New York, 1998), 289, 290, 291, 313.

teacher, by venturing "the hypothesis that blacks might be as competent as whites," ignites a "spark" in her, touches "a nerve that had never been touched before," causing her to be "deeply bothered by the whole race question, ashamed and terrified at the same time"; Yates when she attends a Methodist youth conference in Mississippi and hears a speech by a national church official, an African American dressed in suit and tie—"the first black man I had ever heard speak educated English"—and realizes "Here is a man I want to *be like, not marry, be like.*" After the speech Yates asks a young black woman if she has seen a play then in production at Meridian Junior College and is shocked (though she should not have been) by the answer: "No, well you see, they wouldn't let us in." "And it was in that instant," Yates adds, "that I understood racism. . . . It was at that moment that I was 'converted' to change myself and others with whom I might have influence to overcome the conventional rigidity of my society."[9]

One finds, then, the language of religious conversion in all these narratives, as in their predecessors. Neilson gives the titles "Baptism" and "Awakening" to those sections in which, racially, she sees the light. Indeed, Neilson's story, from racially conventional white Mississippi schoolgirl to press secretary for a black Mississippi congressional candidate, is one of the most intriguing of this second or third generation of conversion narratives—and by one of the youngest of southern converts who have written books on the subject. Born in 1958 to a family of some local prominence, educated in segregation academies, Neilson experiences the beginnings of her racial awakening in a manner that might happen only in Mississippi: in her freshman year at the University of Mississippi she does not get a bid from her sorority of choice and, thus excluded from the social mainstream of campus life, comes to know the meaning of rejection. To those unacquainted with the folkways of the Magnolia State, a rejection from Chi Omega hardly compares with the great rejections in southern letters— Thomas Sutpen's, say, as he is turned away from the front door of a Tidewater mansion, Ellison's Invisible Man's as he is dismissed from his college paradise, or Scarlett's by Rhett at the end of *Gone with the Wind.* But to

9. Melany Neilson, *Even Mississippi* (Tuscaloosa, 1989), 13; Margaret Jones Bolsterli, *Born in the Delta: Reflections on the Making of a Southern White Sensibility* (Knoxville, 1991), 73–74; Gayle Graham Yates, *Mississippi Mind: A Personal Cultural History of an American State* (Knoxville, 1990), 274–75.

Neilson, at the time, it meant everything. Rejected by the society she had aspired to, having "let [her] family down," she finds herself "on the outside," a strange and, soon, strangely attractive position. She comes to know African American students, writes her M.A. thesis on race, and goes to work for black politician Robert Clark. Experiencing her first full "immersion" in a black crowd at a political rally—"shocking and total, like a plunge into icy waters"—and her first visit to a black juke joint, she feels "strange, sickened . . . long[s] to be home." But she stays with the Clark campaign through a victory in the Democratic primary and a close loss in the general election, and then, overwhelmed by the defeat and the racism that contributed to it, she concludes, "I had to get out of Mississippi."[10] Her sentiment was precisely that voiced twenty-five years earlier by a similarly disillusioned Elizabeth Spencer—as well as by Willie Morris, who, as Neilson was leaving Mississippi in 1982, had recently returned home, this time for good.

Both Neilson and Bolsterli, following the pattern of numerous other southern daughters, experience their greatest racial conflicts with their fathers. But Neilson's father, though angry over racial upheaval in the 1960s and upset over her decision to work for a black congressional candidate, eventually changes his position—and thus *Even Mississippi* becomes a narrative at least as much about the conversion of the father as of the daughter. Through his daughter's involvement in civil rights, Ed Tye Neilson goes from defiant segregationist to vocal supporter not only of his daughter's course of action but of her black candidate, and he loses friends and business in the process. Bolsterli's father, at least as he appears in her narrative, experiences no such transformation. He refuses—in the 1950s—to let his daughter realize her "life-long ambition" of attending the University of Chicago because she would have to attend classes "with black people; he meant, of course, black *men*." Bolsterli was disturbed even more by her "most searing [racial] memory," the refusal of her planter father to pay for the use of an incubator for a black baby, the infant child of the family's cook, who was also young Margaret's closest confidante. A doctor's pronouncement that the baby would die without incubation had no effect on her father; as he told his daughter, "Why, honey, I never even heard of

10. Neilson, *Even Mississippi,* 53, 2, 120.

putting a nigra baby in an incubator." That incident "changed things" between Bolsterli and her father: "I never stopped loving him, but I never saw him in quite the same way after that."[11]

Such a father-daughter conflict is also at work in Mab Segrest's *Memoir of a Race Traitor* (1994), the story of an Alabama woman who comes to challenge her racial legacy. Coming of age in the 1950s and 1960s, Segrest cannot help but notice what is happening around her: her father organizes a network of segregation academies in Alabama; her distant cousin, Marvin Segrest, slays a black student activist, Sammy Younge; her Methodist church in Tuskegee turns away African Americans who try to integrate the church. But Segrest's narrative is about far more than race. Writing in the 1990s, she is able to discuss one other aspect of the South's tangled culture of exclusion that Lillian Smith and Katharine Du Pre Lumpkin, bold as they were in their pronouncements a half-century earlier, could not bring themselves to address in any manner remotely personal:

A decade after Marvin shot Sammy at the Tuskegee Greyhound station, I recognized I was lesbian, a self that I first fled and only later came to celebrate. Two decades after Younge's murder, I heard a call, clear as a bell, to oppose the white supremacist forces that kill both "niggers" and "queers." As I did that work, I re-read the biography of Sammy Younge's life in my hometown, finding in his angers, fears and resolves a deeper understanding of my own outcast self.[12]

It should not have taken so long, one might argue, for students of the southern mind to identify in print those close links between racism and homophobia—since both racial integration and homosexuality constituted threats to established roles of race and gender that the South, even more than most societies, held sacred. Segrest, feeling deeply and personally that link, breaks the silence that Smith and Lumpkin could never break.

11. Bolsterli, *Born in the Delta*, 128, 74, 75.

12. Mab Segrest, *Memoir of a Race Traitor* (Boston, 1994), 2. See also Minnie Bruce Pratt, *Rebellion: Essays, 1980–1991* (Ithaca, 1991), for another narrative with Alabama origins that connects racism and homophobia. Pratt writes that her love for another woman, and the disapproval she felt from society because of that love, "led me directly . . . to work against racism and anti-Semitism" (36). Although Pratt acknowledges her debt to Lillian Smith—and *Rebellion* shows Smith's influence—she is also critical of Smith for not having openly discussed her own sexuality.

Not only, in late-century southern memoir, does race intersect with gender and sexuality; it also intersects in a somewhat new and curious manner with class. I say somewhat new because links between race and class have long been recognized and explored not only by southern historians but also by various freelance students of the southern mind. W. J. Cash and many others have observed the manner in which the privileged southern classes have used white racial solidarity—the proto-Dorian bond, in Cash's memorable phrase—to keep poor whites in economic and political bondage, have turned poor southern whites into the militant wing of white racism, those who committed racial atrocities and supplied the Ku Klux Klan with willing and eager recruits. Such a view—that the most virulent southern racism existed among lower-class whites—has been assumed in nearly all the white racial narratives I have discussed. "The greater part of our race prejudice is vested in the lower classes," Sarah Patton Boyle had written—or, in the words of Virginia Durr, those "common as pig tracks."[13] Nearly all of those narratives were written either by sons and daughters of southern privilege, those whose ancestors not only owned slaves but, in most cases, a large number of slaves—Smith, Lumpkin, Boyle, Dabbs, Durr, and so forth—or by those, such as Morris, Watters, and Price, who were at least comfortably middle class. Only Will Campbell and Larry L. King, of the writers I have discussed, might be said to have come from the South's white lower class—and both of them, relatively speaking, from the upper reaches of that class.

Contemporary literary scholars, of course (including those of the American South), hold forth magisterially on that critical triumvirate—race, class, and gender—but, in fact, it is clear that of the three, class has been the least openly and honestly addressed. Such (particularly in recent years) has certainly been the case in discussions of southern fiction, and such is also the case in most discussions of southern memoir and autobiography. One reason is that class is far harder to objectify than race and gender, more difficult to classify with any certainty, and particularly in a region such as the South, which, despite (or perhaps because of) its reputation for class consciousness, has been populated by individuals somewhat uncertain of, thus insecure about, their own class status. In the South, that is (as, to some

13. Boyle, *The Desegregated Heart,* 208; and Durr, *Outside the Magic Circle,* 314.

extent, elsewhere in the United States), one's social class is often defined in part by oneself, and usually to one's own advantage: if one has family (meaning old family), class means family; if one has money, it means money; if one has education and refinement (which usually, but not always, accompany old family)—and does not murder the King's English—it means good taste and proper English. And so forth.

That is one problem in approaching a discussion of class. Another is that of all the southerners who would tell their own stories but have been silenced—by race, class, or gender—the lower-class white has, until recently, been the most effectively silenced. Privileged, lettered southerners have written *about* and occasionally even for poor whites: Faulkner and Flannery O'Connor did, James Agee did, Erskine Caldwell, in his manner, did; even those as far back as the Southwestern Humorists and, long before them, William Byrd, did. But rarely did poor whites speak for themselves. To borrow a metaphor: the abolitionist Wendell Phillips once wrote Frederick Douglass, alluding to the fable of "The Man and the Lion," that the lion would not be so misrepresented "when the lions wrote history."[14] That lion, Douglass, indeed wrote history in the form of his *Narrative* and other autobiographical works. And so, in recent years, have other lions begun to write history; or, to place the matter within the present context, we have Agee's *Let Us Now Praise Famous Men* told not from Agee's point of view but rather from that of his tenant-farmer subjects—or, more precisely, the children and grandchildren of those subjects. Poor southern whites have begun to tell their own stories, not only in fiction but recently, and just as powerfully, in memoir. And much of what they have revealed of their feelings about race is not, in all instances, what those who wrote southern history—those who wrote and abstracted the southern mind—thought had been the case. Nor have they always played the roles that Patty Boyle and Virginia Durr assigned them.

I think of two recent southern memoirs, Tim McLaurin's *Keeper of the Moon* (1991) and Rick Bragg's *All Over but the Shoutin'* (1997), as well as one of several years ago, Harry Crews's *A Childhood: The Biography of a Place* (1978). I could also add Paul Hemphill's *Leaving Birmingham: Notes*

14. Wendell Phillips to Frederick Douglass, 22 April 1845, in Douglass, *Narrative of the Life of Frederick Douglass*, 43.

of a Native Son (1993), Dennis Covington's *Salvation on Sand Mountain*
(1995), and several other recent works.[15] All of these narratives, told by
white southerners who grew up rural poor or urban working class, qualify
more as "class memoir" than race memoir. All of them deal with race, but
not in the same manner as Lillian Smith, Lumpkin, Dabbs, Boyle, and the
other memoirists I have discussed. Crews, McLaurin, Bragg, and Hemphill
could hardly be said to have written racial conversion narratives, and that
fact in itself is instructive: these southerners who grew up socially and (in
most cases) economically disadvantaged, realizing later that they too were
manipulated by the South's upper classes, are hardly in a position to be
overwhelmed by their own racial guilt, thus seem not to have the *need* to repent of racial sins. Or perhaps they feel racial guilt is an indulgence they
cannot afford.

This is not to say they too do not acknowledge, at some point, their earlier mistreatment of African Americans—although, in fact, that mistreatment, in almost all cases, seems to have taken a more benign form than that
of the privileged southerners discussed earlier. Sometimes Crews and
McLaurin played jokes on black children, and Hemphill and Bragg on occasion threw rocks at blacks. And they all grew up violating that most sacro-
sanct rule of southern gentility: they and their families all said "nigger."
The word, Bragg wrote, "was as much a part of the vocabulary as 'hey,' or
'pass the peas.'" That, in the view of the southern racial paternalists of
good family, might have been the greatest offense of all; as Robert Penn
Warren once wrote, "If one of the children in our house had used the word
nigger, the roof would have fallen."[16] The same would have been true in the

15. See also Carl Elliott, *The Cost of Courage: The Journey of an American Congressman*
(New York, 1992) for another autobiography by a poor southerner, born in a log dwelling
on a tenant farm, who went on to serve sixteen years as an Alabama congressman before losing in the 1964 Goldwater sweep of the Deep South. Elliott's childhood, as he describes it,
was characterized by a racial tolerance foreign to many of the more privileged racial converts
I have discussed. Another southerner who defies class/race stereotypes is P. D. East, who
grew up in a series of Mississippi sawmill camps, endured taunts of "nigger-lover" as a teenager (89), and went on to a career as an iconoclastic editor in Mississippi. East tells his story
in *The Magnolia Jungle: The Life, Times and Education of a Southern Editor* (1960).

16. Rick Bragg, *All Over but the Shoutin'* (New York, 1997), 61; and Warren, *Who
Speaks for the Negro?,* 11. *All Over but the Shoutin'* hereafter cited in the text by page
number.

homes of Lillian Smith, Katharine Du Pre Lumpkin, James McBride Dabbs, Sarah Patton Boyle, Virginia Durr, Elizabeth Spencer, Reynolds Price, and Pat Watters: it is notable that the author of nearly every conversion narrative lets the reader know early whether he or she, as a child, used the word "nigger" or not. (The above writers did not; Will Campbell and Larry L. King did.) And with good reason: the word—encoded with racial insensitivity and surliness—carries power of an especially ugly and virulent sort, as American cultural episodes from the periodic banning of *Huckleberry Finn* to the trial of O. J. Simpson assure us. But I am not altogether certain—in the cases of white southerners growing up in the early and mid-twentieth century—whether its use signified a racism any more malignant than that practiced by southerners who did not use it. That is to say, if the memoirs I have considered are any indication, whether one said "nigger" or not seems to have been less a matter of morals than of manners—of *class*. And when a racial convert, in his or her narrative, tells us that he or she did not use the word as a child, he or she is telling us, in a sort of code we are all to recognize, not that he was any less guilty of inhumanity toward African Americans but rather that he came from that most cherished of southern institutions, a good white family.

Crews and McLaurin and Hemphill and Bragg did not come from "good families," and they all said "nigger." All came from backgrounds of no distinction, no education to speak of, and Crews, McLaurin, and Bragg had fathers who sometimes got drunk and mean. They were, that is, Huck Finns far more than they were Quentin Compsons or Isaac McCaslins. But their behavior toward African Americans, as they report it (and in their memoirs they seem to hold nothing back), is in fact less reprehensible—and what's more, is far more *egalitarian*—than that of the more privileged white southerners I have discussed. Crews's childhood friendship with Willalee Bookatee, the black son of a nearby tenant farmer, is closer and on a more equal footing than any friendships the upper-class racial converts had with blacks. "In fantasy," Crews writes, "I often thought of Willalee as my brother, thought of his family as my family." This is hardly to say that Crews, growing up in rural Georgia, was racially color blind. "There was a part of me," he writes, "in which it did not matter at all" that Willalee was black, "but there was another part of me in which it had to matter because it mattered to the world I lived in. It mattered to my blood." Nonetheless, he spent "nearly as much time" with Willalee's family as with his own: "I always felt welcome at his family's house. Whatever I am, they had a large part in making."[17]

McLaurin, too, had a close black friend whose family—equal "socially and economically" to the McLaurins—lived a half mile down the road. He and LJ roamed the woods and fields, and McLaurin stood up for his friend when racial insults came his way. Once when a Croatan Indian well-digger came to the McLaurin farm and brought his two sons along, McLaurin and LJ joined in a dubious act of interracial bonding: both feeling racially superior to the mixed-blood Indians, they taunted and abused the two boys, caused them to fall into a large hole, and then they urinated on them—a "shameful act," McLaurin later realizes, "one that God would write down"—but one undertaken in defense of their joint "home turf." McLaurin's friendship with LJ, however, eventually goes the way of many interracial southern friendships. The breach began one day in the early 1960s when LJ wandered up to find McLaurin and his cousins, inspired by the racist remarks of their fathers, ridiculing Martin Luther King, Jr., and civil rights demonstrators. McLaurin tried to apologize, but to no avail. That "crack in our union against time and change," he writes, was only the first. As McLaurin became aware that "a war was beginning between whites and blacks," and as LJ discovered Black Power, they drew apart. When LJ was murdered twenty years later, beaten to death in what seemed to be a drug deal gone bad, McLaurin and his brother attended the funeral: "We were the only white people there, as his father was the only black person to attend my father's funeral." More than Crews, McLaurin acknowledges his racial transgressions. But confession and racial conversion are far from his primary concerns, repentance of that or any other variety, he suggests, not being in his line.[18]

If Crews's and McLaurin's narratives have echoes of *Huckleberry Finn*, complete with interracial friendship, a father given to drinking binges, and the narrator's refusal to be "sivilized," Rick Bragg's *All Over but the Shoutin'* is the leading twentieth-century, true-to-life contender for that

---

17. Harry Crews, *A Childhood: The Biography of a Place* (New York, 1978), 68, 57, 62.

18. Tim McLaurin, *Keeper of the Moon* (New York, 1991), 114, 124, 121, 119, 310, 38–40.

honor. Growing up in the 1960s and early 1970s in the hills of northern Alabama, a resourceful kid with a mean drunk for a father, Bragg was aware that he and his family were looked down on by all, white and black, as "poor white trash." Like Huck, for better or worse, Bragg is cut off from what most would call respectable institutions. He had, in his early years, "seldom been anywhere close" to churches: "my daddy had not believed in them" (81). And he tells his story in Huck's straightforward, unassuming manner, suspicious of "books" and those who read and interpret them: "No, this is not an important book. The people who know about books call it a memoir, but that is much too fancy a word for me" (xxi).

But a memoir Bragg's story is, and when it appeared in 1997 it found itself in a tradition, if a very recent one, of remarkable working-class Alabama memoirs—which is to say, not Virginia Durr's Alabama of Black Belt privilege and racial paternalism but George Wallace's hardscrabble Alabama, devoid both of privilege and paternalism. Dennis Covington's *Salvation on Sand Mountain* (1995), which appeared just before Bragg's book, was principally about snake handling, although, as Covington writes, he took up snakes partly "in order to conquer the metaphorical snake," racism, "that was my cultural legacy": "When I was growing up . . . among families reaching for the middle class, the past was problematic and embarrassing because it contained poverty, ignorance, racism, and defeat. The legacy of Southern history was as dangerous as any rattlesnake." Similarly, Paul Hemphill wrote *Leaving Birmingham* (1993) in order to come to terms with his cultural and racial legacy. Growing up in the 1940s, Hemphill belonged to a family, down from the hills, that was no longer hardscrabble poor—his father made a good living as a truck driver—but the Hemphills, like the Covingtons, lived in a blue-collar Birmingham neighborhood and had all the prejudices presumed to be requisite for their class. *Leaving Birmingham,* in fact, is one working-class memoir that *does* support the assumption that the white lower class is the repository of the most virulent brand of southern racism—in Hemphill's case, not so much his own as that of his father. And beginning in the late 1940s, when Paul, Jr., was in his early teens, the racism of Paul Hemphill, Sr., began to take on a meaner edge; instead of talking baseball with his son, he began to talk racial hatred. As the son was awakened to his own racial sins—awakened in the early 1960s by Birmingham's hostile reception to the Freedom Riders, then the bombing of the Sixteenth Street Baptist Church—he found himself increasingly alienated from his father, who now "sounded like a Klansman," and who finally "was eaten up by racism as though it were a cancer."[19]

Hemphill's own journey up from racism (though he never actually speaks of *conversion* in the manner of many of the racially born again) was aided by his exposure to a larger world—college, semipro baseball (where his best friend was a black outfielder), an air force stint in Europe, sportswriting in Birmingham and other southern outposts, then other newspaper jobs and a Nieman Fellowship at Harvard. It was a journey that, in many ways, anticipated that, twenty years later, of Rick Bragg—who also escaped the north Alabama hills, and a life much bleaker than Hemphill's, through sports, sportswriting, eventually college, newspaper jobs in Birmingham and around the South and, as with Hemphill, a Nieman Fellowship—with, in Bragg's case, a Pulitzer Prize for feature writing thrown in for good measure. But Bragg sees his own achievements as being no more remarkable than those of his mother, and he tells his story, he writes in the beginning of his book, to let her know that *she* was a success: "I am . . . just as proud of being the son of a woman who picked cotton and took in ironing as I am of working for a place like the *New York Times*" (xx).

The beginning of Bragg's journey was an unpromising one, complete with outhouse, welfare checks, and other trappings of rural poverty. Bragg's father, as his son describes him, was indeed a twentieth-century version of Pap Finn, "a fearsome man, the kind of slim and lethal Southern man who would react with murderous fury when insulted, attacking with a knife or a pine knot or his bare hands" (7). Like Pap, Bragg's father is fond of moonshine and, like Pap, in his last days, he begins to see a death angel—in his case, "a dark angel, perched like a crow on the footboard of his bed, just waiting, expectant" (7). And Rick resembles Huck in ways other than having a drunken, abusive father who frequently abandons him—although Bragg, of course, never mentions Huck or the resemblance, since to do so would be self-consciously literary in a manner the author takes great pains to avoid. But he reinforces the resemblance to Huck by lapsing into the col-

---

19. Dennis Covington, *Salvation on Sand Mountain: Snake Handling and Redemption in Southern Appalachia* (New York, 1995), 152–53, 151; and Paul Hemphill, *Leaving Birmingham: Notes of a Native Son* (New York, 1993), 132, 188.

loquial and, at times, the ungrammatical. Like Huck, Rick is a realist: "I believed what I could see and hear and sometimes what I could feel" (86). Like Huck, he doesn't put much stock in formal religion: after his father abandons the family and his mother decides to send Rick to church, "I . . . stomped and rolled my eyes and even said 'damn' under my breath at the prospect of church" (83). When he does attend and hears the preacher issue a call for salvation, he waits for "the invasion, the infusion, the joy . . . for the Holy Ghost to slip inside my heart and my mind." But he waits in vain: "I just sat there. . . . I had never felt so alone before. . . . I don't think I ever have, since" (88).

Bragg is suspicious of conversions of any sort, including racial ones, although he fully recognizes the evils of the society that bred him. Although geographically and sociologically detached from most African Americans—"I was not of a world where there were maids, cooks or servants. . . . There were no black people in my school and at that time no black person had ever been in my house or in my yard" (59)—he hears his uncles and cousins speak of "the nigger trouble" (58) and listens as George Wallace "tell[s] us we are better than the nigras" (61). Both blacks and whites, Bragg later realizes, suffered in the rural South, both were "wanting and desperate," but they were "kept separate by hard men who hid their faces under hoods and their deeds under some twisted interpretation of the Bible, and kicked the living shit out of anyone who thought it should be different" (4–5). In his youth, "the orange fires of shacks and crosses lit up the evening sky" (5).

Bragg writes that he knew no black people, but in fact he did have a "few contacts" with a black family who lived nearby: "we had thrown rocks at them." He knew only one of the black children by name—"he had some kind of brain condition that caused tremendous swelling in his head. The others called him Water Head" (66)—and once, after Bragg had bounced a rock off his back, he'd heard the boy cry out. That was the extent of his acquaintance, a fact that made all the more improbable an experience that "ultimately shaped and softened my own family." The incident occurred in the 1960s, during an especially dark chapter in southern racial history, "a year of burning buses and Klan picnics" (62), "a time of horrors, in Birmingham, in the backwoods of Mississippi . . . a time when the whole damn world seemed on fire" (66). It was also a time of crisis in Bragg's family, "the darkest and ugliest time of my childhood" (62). His father had taken off, his mother's credit had run out, the family was nearly out of food; in every way, "we were at rock bottom" (65). And "in the midst of it, in the middle of the hating and fear," as well as the deprivation, came "a simple kindness from the most unexpected place, from people who had no reason, beyond their own common decency, to reach across that fence of hate that so many people worked so hard to build" (62). One day one of the children, "the color of bourbon," from down the road knocked at their door: "He said his momma had some corn left over and please, ma'am, would we like it?" (65).

The tortured logic of southern racial etiquette might lead one to believe that the Braggs would decline the gift, that they would refuse to be put in a situation in which they had fallen so far they would have to accept help from a black family. But, hungry and hopeless, they took the food with gratitude. "It may seem like a little bitty thing by 1990s reasoning," Bragg adds. "But this was a time when beatings were common, when it was routine, out of pure meanness, to take a young black man for a ride and leave him cut, broken or worse on the side of some pulpwood road. For sport. For fun" (65–66). Bragg is careful not to overplay the incident. Although he would "like to say that we came together, after the little boy brought us that food, that we learned about and from each other," that "would be a lie." This was, after all, rural Alabama in 1965, "two separate distinct states." But "at least, we didn't throw no more rocks" (66).

That was Bragg the realist, and a realist he remained. Concrete needs and deprivations meant vastly more than the abstraction of family honor or any of those other abstractions—including the most monstrous of all, racial segregation—by which more privileged southerners, and the least privileged too, often lived. There is little of the romantic in Bragg, no more than there is in Crews, McLaurin, or Hemphill, no more than in Huck, and not much of the sentimentalist either. The nearest Bragg ever comes to the luxury of self-indulgence is when, after covering a Miami race riot and fleeing from rocks thrown at him, he keeps a rock that hits him. "Once, when I looked at it," he writes in an earlier draft of his book, "I thought of Waterhead, the little boy from Spring Garden I had hit in the back so long ago. Wherever you are, hoss, I thought to myself, I'm sorry." That is a close as Bragg ever comes to racial guilt and repentance—and he cuts that passage in the book's final version.

One remains, one final story by a self-proclaimed poor white who did in fact mix a grim southern realism of poverty and failure with a particularly intoxicating brand of romanticism, the romanticism of white robe and hood and burning cross—another story told by a downtrodden white southerner that, this time, does become a conversion narrative, indeed perhaps the quintessential racial conversion narrative. C. P. Ellis of Durham, North Carolina, son of a heavy-drinking textile worker who was often out of a job, had grown up so poor and had worn clothes so old that he left school every afternoon "with a sense of inferiority," a feeling that people were "makin' fun of me."[20] Quitting school after the eighth grade, he tried a number of jobs but couldn't get ahead. Bitter, not knowing whom to blame but having "to hate somebody," he decides that "the natural person for me to hate would be black people" (202). Like his father before him, he joins the Ku Klux Klan, and he rises to exalted cyclops (president) of the Durham Klan before, in spite of himself, he is thrust into a situation in which he has to associate with blacks. Attending a school desegregation meeting to make sure the Klan point of view is represented, he finds himself elected co-chair of an interracial group; then, after realizing how much poor blacks and poor whites have in common, he experiences a racial transformation that he calls being "born again" (209). Such is the bare outline of the story C. P. Ellis tells, although he tells his story in something other than the conventional manner. He tells it to a tape recorder, and it finds its way into Studs Terkel's *American Dreams: Lost and Found* (1981). But it is Ellis's own story, in Ellis's own words, and if he himself had written it down and given it a title, he might have called it what Thomas Tarrants, two years earlier, had titled his narrative of racial transformation, *The Conversion of a Klansman.*

Somewhat in the manner of seventeenth-century Puritans, Ellis proclaims himself the greatest of sinners—of racial sinners, in his case—and his claim to that title is better than most. On one occasion he had approached a young black man, pulled out his pistol, put it "right at his head," and said, "I've always wanted to kill a nigger and I think I'll make

20. C. P. Ellis [oral history], in Studs Terkel, *American Dreams: Lost and Found* (London, 1981), 201. Hereafter cited in the text by page number.

you the first one" (204); on another occasion he did shoot a black man and was arrested but acquitted; on still another occasion, when he heard news of the assassination of Martin Luther King, he got together a party of Klansmen, "really rejoicin' cause that son of a bitch was dead" (211). Ellis tells this and more, but he also comes to *understand* his racism far better than most other racial converts. Although he had come by it honestly—from his father—his racial hatred did not become pronounced until, in his twenties, married with four children, he found himself working as hard as he could, pumping gas, working a bread route, then borrowing money to buy a gas station—working "all the overtime I could get and still could not survive financially. . . . It just kept gettin' worse and worse" (201–02). In a "hole," becoming "really . . . bitter," and needing someone to blame, he "began to blame it on black people." "I had to hate somebody," he explains. "Hatin' America is hard to do because you can't see it to hate it. You gotta have somethin' to look at to hate" (202).

It was shortly after reaching this conclusion that C. P. Ellis joined the Klan, and soon he was elected chaplain, then vice-president, and finally exalted cyclops. The night he became a Klansman was particularly memorable:

> I was led into a large meeting room, and this was the time of my life! It was thrilling. Here's a guy who's worked all his life and struggled all his life to be something, and here's the moment to be something. I will never forget it. Four robed Klansmen led me into the hall. The lights were dim, and the only thing you could see was an illuminated cross. I knelt before the cross. I had to make certain vows and promises. We promised to uphold the purity of the white race, fight communism, and protect white womanhood. (203)

That experience, before his other conversion, his racial one, was a kind of conversion in itself, as Ellis knelt before the cross. After he took his oath, he heard "loud applause goin' throughout the buildin', musta been at least four hundred people. . . . It was a thrilling moment for C. P. Ellis" (203).

Ellis's initiation into the brotherhood of racial hatred was enthusiastic and dramatic; his conversion to racial brotherhood was to come far more slowly and reluctantly. After plunging into Klan activities with all the zeal of a new convert—organizing a Klan youth group, holding weekly meetings with students, "teachin' the principles of the Klan" (203)—he also started showing up at Durham city council meetings in order to voice his opposition to black demands. But gradually he became aware that white councilmen were using both him and his black opponents for their own ends. Privately, they would phone him, asking him to continue to voice his opposition to black demands, but publicly they would have nothing to do with him. This realization hit him particularly hard one day on a downtown street when "a certain city council member saw me comin'." Ellis expected the man to shake his hand—"because he was talkin' with me at night on the telephone" and "I had been in his home and visited with him"—but the councilman crossed the street to avoid him. "That's when I began to do some real serious thinkin'," Ellis explains. What he decided was that as long as well-off whites "kept low-income whites and low-income blacks fightin'," they were going to "maintain control." And after being ignored in public, he decided "you're not gonna use me any more" (205).

It was a long way from that declaration to full-scale racial conversion. "I still didn't like blacks," Ellis recalls, but he had begun to look at African Americans in a different way: "I'd go home at night and I'd have to wrestle with myself. I'd look at a black person walkin' down the street, and the guy'd have ragged shoes or his clothes would be worn. That began to do somethin' to me inside" (205). Still, Ellis might not have changed so radically if he had not received a call one night from an AFL-CIO official inviting him to a meeting, supported by a grant from HEW, to deal with racial problems in Durham's public schools. "No way am I comin' with all those niggers," Ellis protested at first, but he decided to go after all, to make sure his point of view was represented. He expressed that view—"If we didn't have niggers in the schools, we wouldn't have the problems we got today" (206)—and, at least as he tells it, he got such high marks for his forthrightness, even from some blacks, that during the next meeting he was elected co-chair of the interracial committee, along with a militant black woman, Ann Atwater, with whom he had earlier had confrontations: "How I just hated that black nigger" (204). In spite of his "hatred for blacks and Jews and liberals," he accepted the job: "Her and I began to reluctantly work together" (207).

Such was the unlikely beginning of Ellis's transformation, but as he works with Atwater he begins to experience that same sense of racial betrayal that converts from Huck Finn forward had experienced. His friends told him he was "sellin' out the white race," and he wondered if they might be right:

> This begin to make me have guilt feelin's. Am I doin' right? Am I doin' wrong? Here I am all of a sudden makin' an about-face and tryin' to deal with my feelin's, my heart. My mind was beginnin' to open up. I was beginnin' to see what was right and what was wrong. (207)

The "guilt feelin's," then, were of two kinds—first the guilt he felt for betraying his old Klan friends, but also, increasingly, guilt over his own many racial transgressions. As he works with Atwater, he comes to see that her problems and those of other poor blacks are the same as his:

> The whole world was openin' up, and I was learnin' new truths that I had never learned before. I was beginning to look at a black person, shake hands with him, and see him as a human bein'. I hadn't got rid of all this stuff. I've still got a little bit of it. But somethin' was happenin' to me. (209)

It was "a new life," Ellis recalls: "I didn't have those sleepless nights I used to have when I was active in the Klan." It was "almost like bein' born again" (209).

Ellis's life changes in ways he had never thought possible. Working in the maintenance department at Duke University, he begins to attend high school in the afternoon—"I was about the only white in class, and the oldest" (209)—and he sticks with it until he graduates. Previously antiunion, now he runs for the office of union business manager, runs against a black man, gains the support of the predominantly black union, and wins overwhelmingly. Increasingly he sees the world not in terms of race but of class. He thinks again of the Durham councilman who had crossed the street to avoid shaking hands with him. He recalls the reception he had received on another occasion from the white mayor of Durham—condescending, a bit amused. He quits the Klan but he still defends Klansmen: "The majority of 'em are low-income whites, people who really don't have a part in something. They have been shut out as well as the blacks. . . . Deep down inside, we want to be part of this great society. Nobody listens, so we join these groups" (203). It is a bond of poor people, black and white, in which Ellis finally believes, and, telling his story at age fifty-two, he discovers he himself has lived an "impossible dream." People tell him he "sound[s] like Martin Luther King," and he agrees. In 1968 he had cheered King's death. Now, only a decade later, "since I changed," he sits and listens to tapes of King's speeches: "I listen to it and tears come to my eyes 'cause I know what he's saying now. I know what's happenin' " (211).

One might be tempted to conclude that Ellis's narrative is altogether artless, altogether unselfconscious. In fact, even an oral history has its artifice: Ellis clearly knows he has a good story, he knows how to tell it, and he enjoys telling it. There is no doubt, however, of the genuineness of his racial transformation, no doubt that his story of that transformation is, in many respects, even more compelling than those literary narratives by Smith, Lumpkin, Dabbs, Boyle, and other representatives of southern high culture. As Ellis tells his story, both he and his narrative are still works in progress. Unlike the other authors I have considered, he has not, as the world would measure him, risen very far. Unlike even those other memoirists of humble origins—Crews, McLaurin, Hemphill, and Bragg—he has barely risen. As they tell their stories, they are, after all, successful writers; they have arrived. Ellis, economically, socially, educationally, culturally, is still near the bottom, fighting the forces of race and class oppression: "I still got some of those inferiority feelin's now that I have to overcome once in a while" (201). That notwithstanding, the story of his spiritual triumph, his transformation from Klansman to racial brotherhood, lies more squarely at that treacherous intersection of race and class than any of the others I have considered. And it is at that intersection, fraught with paradoxes and contradictions, that any honest discussion of contemporary southern life increasingly must lie.

BIBLIOGRAPHY

Abbott, Shirley. *The Bookmaker's Daughter.* New York, 1991.

———. *Womenfolks: Growing Up Down South.* New York, 1983.

Allison, Dorothy. *Two or Three Things I Know for Sure.* New York, 1995.

Ashmore, Harry S. *Hearts and Minds: The Anatomy of Racism from Roosevelt to Reagan.* New York, 1982.

Ball, Edward. *Slaves in the Family.* New York, 1998.

Berry, Wendell. *The Hidden Wound.* Boston, 1970.

Blair, Lewis Harvie. *A Southern Prophecy: The Prosperity of the South Dependent upon the Elevation of the Negro.* Edited with an Introduction by C. Vann Woodward. Boston, 1964.

Blotner, Joseph L., and Frederick L. Gwynn, eds. *Faulkner in the University.* Charlottesville, 1959.

Bolsterli, Margaret Jones. *Born in the Delta: Reflections on the Making of a Southern White Sensibility.* Knoxville, 1991.

Boyle, Sarah Patton. *The Desegregated Heart.* New York, 1962.

Braden, Anne. *The Wall Between.* New York, 1958.

Bragg, Rick. *All Over but the Shoutin'.* New York, 1997.

Brantley, Will. *Feminine Sense in Southern Memoir.* Jackson, Miss., 1993.

Cable, George W. "My Politics." In *The Negro Question: A Selection of Writings on Civil Rights in the South.* Edited by Arlin Turner. New York, 1958.

Caldwell, Patricia. *The Puritan Conversion Narrative: The Beginnings of American Expression.* New York, 1983.

Campbell, Will. *Brother to a Dragonfly.* 1977. Reprint. New York, 1994.

———. *Forty Acres and a Goat.* Atlanta, 1986.

———. *Providence.* Atlanta, 1992.

———. *Race and the Renewal of the Church.* Philadelphia, 1962.

———. *The Stem of Jesse.* Macon, Ga., 1995.

Carter, Hodding. "Hope in the South." *Saturday Review,* 2 April 1955, p. 35.

———. *Southern Legacy.* Baton Rouge, 1950.

Cash, W. J. *The Mind of the South.* New York, 1941.

Clayton, Bruce. *The Savage Ideal: Intolerance and Intellectual Leadership in the South, 1890–1914.* Baltimore, 1972.

Cohen, Charles Lloyd. *God's Caress: The Psychology of Puritan Religious Experience.* New York, 1986.

Covington, Dennis. *Salvation on Sand Mountain: Snake Handling and Redemption in Southern Appalachia.* New York, 1995.

Cox, James M. "Between Defiance and Defense: Owning Up to the South." In *Located Lives: Place and Idea in Southern Autobiography.* Edited by J. Bill Berry. Athens, Ga., 1990.

Crews, Harry. *A Childhood: The Biography of a Place.* New York, 1978.

Cunnigen, Donald. "Men and Women of Goodwill: Mississippi's White Liberals." Ph.D. dissertation, Harvard University, 1988.

Dabbs, James McBride. *Haunted By God.* Richmond, 1972.

———. *The Road Home.* Philadelphia, 1960.

———. *The Southern Heritage.* New York, 1958.

———. *Who Speaks for the South?* New York, 1964.

Dabney, Robert Lewis. *A Defence of Virginia and Through Her of the South.* New York, 1867.

———. *The New South.* Raleigh, 1883.

Dabney, Virginius. *Below the Potomac: A Book About the New South.* New York, 1942.

Daniels, Jonathan. *A Southerner Discovers the South.* New York, 1938.

Danner, Dorothy. *The Confessions of Dorothy Danner.* Edited by Richard A. Pride. Nashville, 1995.

Davis, David Brion. *The Problem of Slavery in the Age of Revolution, 1770–1823.* Ithaca, 1975.

Degler, Carl N. *The Other South: Southern Dissenters in the Nineteenth Century.* New York, 1974.

Dorsey, Peter A. *Sacred Estrangement: The Rhetoric of Conversion in Modern American Autobiography.* University Park, Pa., 1993.

Douglas, Ellen. *Truth: Four Stories I Am Finally Old Enough to Tell.* Chapel Hill, 1998.

Douglass, Frederick. *Narrative of the Life of Frederick Douglass.* 1845. Reprint. New York, 1982.

Durr, Virginia. *Outside the Magic Circle: The Autobiography of Virginia Foster Durr.* Edited by Hollinger F. Barnard. Tuscaloosa, 1985.

East, P. D. *The Magnolia Jungle: The Life, Times and Education of a Southern Editor.* New York, 1960.

[Edwards, Jonathan.] *The Great Awakening.* Edited with Introduction by C. C. Goen. New Haven, 1972.

———. "A Narrative of Surprising Conversions." In *Jonathan Edwards on Revival.* [n.c.] 1984.

Egerton, John. *A Mind to Stay Here: Profiles from the South.* New York, 1970.

———. *Speak Now Against the Day: The Generation Before the Civil Rights Movement in the South.* New York, 1994.

Elliott, Carl. *The Cost of Courage: The Journey of an American Congressman.* New York, 1992.

Ellis, C. P. [oral history]. In Studs Terkel, *American Dreams: Lost and Found.* London, 1981.

Evans, Eli N. *The Lonely Days Were Sundays.* Jackson, Miss., 1993.

———. *The Provincials: A Personal History of the Jews in the South.* New York, 1973.

Faulkner, William. "The Bear." In *The Portable Faulkner.* Edited by Malcolm Cowley. 1946. Revised edition. New York, 1967.

Fox-Genovese, Elizabeth. "Between Individualism and Community: Autobiographies of Southern Women." In *Located Lives: Place and Idea in Southern Autobiography.* Edited by J. Bill Berry. Athens, Ga., 1990.

Gladney, Margaret Rose, ed. *How Am I To Be Heard?: Letters of Lillian Smith.* Chapel Hill, 1993.

Gore, Albert. *Let the Glory Out: My South and Its Politics.* New York, 1972.

Griffin, John Howard. *Black Like Me.* Boston, 1961.

Gura, Philip F. *A Glimpse of Sion's Glory: Puritan Radicalism in New England, 1620–1660.* Middletown, Conn., 1984.

Hall, Jacquelyn Dowd. "Katharine Du Pre Lumpkin." *American National Biography.* Edited by John A. Garraty. New York. Forthcoming.

———. "Open Secrets: Memory, Imagination, and the Refashioning of Southern Identity." *American Quarterly,* L (March 1998), 109–24.

———. " 'You Must Remember This': Autobiography as Social Critique." *The Journal of American History.* Forthcoming.

Haygood, Atticus. *Our Brother in Black.* Nashville, 1881.

Hays, Brooks. *A Southern Moderate Speaks.* Chapel Hill, 1959.

Hemphill, Paul. *Leaving Birmingham: Notes of a Native Son.* New York, 1993.

Hill, Samuel S., Jr. *The South and the North in American Religion.* Athens, Ga., 1980.

———. "The South's Two Cultures." In Hill, et al., *Religion and the Solid South.* Nashville, 1972.

———. *Southern Churches in Crisis.* New York, 1966.

Hobson, Fred. *Tell About the South: The Southern Rage to Explain.* 1983. Reprint. Baton Rouge, 1998.

Hundley, Daniel R. *Social Relations in Our Southern States.* 1860. Reprint. Baton Rouge, 1979.

Hutchens, John K. "Lillian Smith." *New York Herald Tribune Books,* 30 October 1949, p. 2.

James, William. *The Varieties of Religious Experience.* 1902. Reprint. New York, 1982.

Jefferson, Thomas. *Notes on the State of Virginia.* Edited by William Peden. 1787. Reprint. New York, 1972.

Ketchin, Susan. *The Christ-Haunted Landscape: Faith and Doubt in Southern Fiction.* Jackson, Miss., 1994.

Killian, Lewis M. *Black and White: Reflections of a White Southern Sociologist.* Dix Hill, N.Y., 1994.

King, Florence. *Confessions of a Failed Southern Lady.* New York, 1985.

King, Larry L. *Confessions of a White Racist.* New York, 1971.

———. *None But a Blockhead: On Being a Writer.* New York, 1986.

King, Richard H. *A Southern Renaissance: The Cultural Awakening of the American South, 1930–1955.* New York, 1980.

Loveland, Anne C. *Lillian Smith: A Southerner Confronting the South.* Baton Rouge, 1986.

———. *Southern Evangelicals and the Social Order, 1800–1860.* Baton Rouge, 1980.

Lumpkin, Katharine Du Pre. *The Emancipation of Angelina Grimké.* Chapel Hill, 1974.

———. *The Making of a Southerner.* New York, 1947.

Marsh, Charles. *God's Long Summer: Stories of Faith and Civil Rights.* Princeton, 1997.

Martin, Bernard. *John Newton: A Biography.* London, 1950.

Mather, Cotton. *Paterna: The Autobiography of Cotton Mather.* Edited by Ronald A. Bosco. Delmar, N.Y., 1976.

Mays, John Bentley. *Power in the Blood: Land, Memory and a Southern Family.* New York, 1997.

McGill, Ralph. "A Matter of Change." *New York Times Book Review,* 13 February 1955, p. 7.

——. *The South and the Southerner.* 1963. Reprint. Athens, Ga., 1992.

McLaurin, Melton A. *Separate Pasts: Growing Up White in the Segregated South.* Athens, Ga., 1987.

McLaurin, Tim. *Keeper of the Moon.* New York, 1991.

McMillan, George. "Portrait of a Southern Liberal." *New York Review of Books,* 18 April 1974, p. 33.

Morgan, Edmund S., ed. *The Diary of Michael Wigglesworth, 1653–1657.* Gloucester, Mass., 1965.

Morris, Willie. *The Ghosts of Medgar Evers.* New York, 1998.

——. *Homecomings.* Jackson, Miss., 1989.

——. *New York Days.* Boston, 1993.

——. *North Toward Home.* 1967. Reprint. Oxford, Miss., 1982.

——. *"Terrains of the Heart" and Other Essays on Home.* Oxford, Miss., 1981.

——. *Yazoo: Integration in a Deep South Town.* New York, 1971.

Neilson, Melany. *Even Mississippi.* Tuscaloosa, 1989.

Pratt, Minnie Bruce. *Rebellion: Essays, 1980–1991.* Ithaca, 1991.

Price, Reynolds. *Clear Pictures.* New York, 1989.

Romine, Scott. "Framing Southern Rhetoric: Lillian Smith's Narrative Persona in *Killers of the Dream.*" *South Atlantic Review,* LIX (May 1994), 95–111.

Scott, Anne Firor. *The Southern Lady from Pedestal to Politics.* Chicago, 1970.

——. "Women, Religion, and Social Change." In Samuel S. Hill, Jr., et. al., *Religion and the Solid South.* Nashville, 1972.

Segrest, Mab. *Memoir of a Race Traitor.* Boston, 1994.

Simpson, Lewis P. "The Autobiographical Impulse in the South." In *Home Ground: Southern Autobiography.* Edited by J. Bill Berry. Columbia, Mo., 1991.

Smith, Frank. *Congressman from Mississippi.* New York, 1964.

Smith, Henry Nash. *Mark Twain: The Development of a Writer.* 1962. Reprint. New York, 1972.

Smith, Lillian. *The Journey.* New York, 1954.

——. *Killers of the Dream.* New York, 1949.

——. *Killers of the Dream.* Revised edition. New York, 1961.

——. *Now Is the Time.* New York, 1955.

——. *Our Faces, Our Words.* New York, 1964.

——. *The Winner Names the Age.* Edited by Michelle Cliff. New York, 1978.

Sosna, Morton Philip. *In Search of the Silent South: Southern Liberals and the Race Issue.* New York, 1977.

————. "In Search of the Silent South: White Southern Racial Liberalism, 1920–1950." Ph.D. dissertation, University of Wisconsin, 1973.

Spencer, Elizabeth. *Landscapes of the Heart.* New York, 1998.

Styron, William. "A Horrible Little Racist." *New York Times Magazine,* 8 October 1995, p. 80.

————. "Jimmy in the House." In *James Baldwin: The Legacy.* Edited by Quincy Troupe. New York, 1989.

————. "This Quiet Dust." In *"This Quiet Dust" and Other Writings.* New York, 1982.

Sullivan, Walter. "Strange Children: Caroline Gordon and Allen Tate." In *Home Ground: Southern Autobiography.* Edited by J. Bill Berry. Columbia, Mo., 1991.

Tarrants, Thomas A., III. *The Conversion of a Klansman.* Garden City, N.Y., 1979.

Tate, Allen. "A Lost Traveller's Dream." In *Memoirs and Opinions, 1926–1974.* Chicago, 1975.

Twain, Mark [Samuel Clemens]. *The Adventures of Huckleberry Finn.* 1885. Reprint. New York, 1948.

Warren, Robert Penn. *The Legacy of the Civil War: Meditations on the Centennial.* New York, 1961.

————. *Segregation: The Inner Conflict in the South.* New York, 1956.

————. *Who Speaks for the Negro?* New York, 1965.

Watters, Pat. *Down to Now: Reflections on the Civil Rights Movement.* New York, 1971.

————. *The South and the Nation.* New York, 1969.

Weltner, Charles Longstreet. *Southerner.* Philadelphia, 1966.

Welty, Eudora. *One Writer's Beginnings.* Cambridge, Mass., 1983.

White, Helen, and Redding S. Sugg, Jr. *From the Mountain: Selections from Pseudopodia, the North Georgia Review, and South Today.* Memphis, 1972.

Williamson, Joel. *The Crucible of Race.* New York, 1984.

Winslow, Ola Elizabeth, ed. *Jonathan Edwards: Basic Writings.* New York, 1966.

Woodward, C. Vann, ed. *Mary Chesnut's Civil War.* New Haven, 1981.

Wyatt-Brown, Bertram. *Honor and Violence in the Old South.* New York, 1986.

Wynes, Charles E., ed. *Forgotten Voices: Dissenting Southerners in an Age of Conformity.* Baton Rouge, 1967.

Yates, Gayle Graham. *Mississippi Mind: A Personal Cultural History of an American State.* Knoxville, 1990.

Index